PRAY 21

discovery guide

Timothy Eldred
with Brian Smith

CHRISTIAN ENDEAVOR INTERNATIONAL

PRAY21 DISCOVERY GUIDE
© 2007 Christian Endeavor International
International Standard Book Number: 978-0-9796551-0-4

Cover design by Zeal
Interior design and typeset by Katherine Lloyd, The DESK

Printed in Canada

For information:
Christian Endeavor International
PO Box 377
424 East Main Street
Edmore, MI 48829

Contents

A Word from Timothy Eldred 5

How to Use This Book 7

Part 1: Believe **9**

Day 1: How Many Loaves Do You Have? 10

Day 2: Do You Really Believe I Can Do This? 15

Day 3: Do You Believe in the Son? 20

Day 4: Why Did You Doubt? 25

Day 5: Don't You Know Me Yet? 30

Part 2: Belong **35**

Day 6: Haven't I Handpicked You? 36

Day 7: What Good to Gain the World and Lose Your Soul? 41

  > One-Week Checkpoint 46

Day 8: What's Easier to Fix—Body or Heart? 48

Day 9: Who Loves God More? 53

Day 10: What Are You After? 58

Part 3: Become **63**

Day 11: Are You Really Listening? 64

Day 12: Who Do You Say I Am? 69

Day 13: Who Doesn't First Figure the Cost? 74

Day 14: Do You Want to Get Well? 79

  > Two-Week Checkpoint 84

Day 15: Should I Beg for Escape? 86

Part 4: Be **91**

Day 16: Didn't You Know I Had to Be About My Father's Business? 92

Day 17: Won't God Answer His Children's Persistent Prayers? 97

Day 18: Do You Put a Lamp Under the Bed? 102

Day 19: Do You Really Love Me? 106

Day 20: Are You Able to Drink from the Same Cup as Me? 111

Day 21: Will You Really Die for Me? 116

  > Three-Week Checkpoint 121

Another Word from Timothy 123

Endnotes 125

A Word from Timothy Eldred

It was all I could do not to fail tenth-grade geometry. Tutors and teachers did their best. But I had some kind of mental block, maybe missed some basic concept somewhere in the past.

I got a D.

Minus.

But I got by.

Some questions in life never get answered. But not because they're never asked. Just because of some mental block. Some basic concept missing.

Everything else in my life seemed fine. *Seemed.* Tim had it together. Outgoing. Confident. Successful. Getting by in life. So no one bothered asking the hard questions.

Some questions never get answered because we don't see any reason to ask. If status quo is adequate, why challenge it?

And then there are the questions we're afraid to ask. Afraid of the answers.

Growth begins with good questions. But if the questions never get asked or answered, growth stalls. A lot of people live and die without answers. Getting by.

It's a tragedy to settle for a D-minus in life.

I was thirty-four before someone asked me the question I'd never faced. My mentor asked, "Who are you?"

Silence. He might as easily have asked me to calculate the hypotenuse of a trapezoidal penta-gon. He wasn't just requesting my name, title, or least favorite Disney character. And I knew it. I tried bluffing. He caught me. I only needed to answer the question. I had no idea.

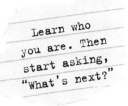

Learn who you are. Then start asking, "What's next?"

When I eventually figured it out, the answer involved some scary soul searching. The kind I'm inviting you to do. In accepting the Pray21 chal-lenge, you're going to hit some hard questions. Maybe you're young. You need to face the *Who are you?* question now, before you waste years pre-tending. (By the way, if you have placed your faith in Christ, you can know with absolute certainty who you are. You'll see what I mean by the end of the book.)

Or perhaps you're not so young. A long way down the road. Career established, family growing, and maybe still unaware of your identity or purpose. (You can know who you are, too. Someone should have helped you figure it out long ago.)

We're all asking the same question. It's not too late to find the answer. And when you find yourself, you'll be able to do *all* God made you to do. And have the time of your life doing it.

You have been created for significance and service, called to mission and ministry. Getting by is not an option. Getting by is getting lost.

In this book you'll read about people like you. Asking questions. Avoiding questions. Oblivious to the questions. People in discovery. Getting beyond just getting by. When you wrestle with their stories, you'll open doors for *your* journey of discovery. Maybe you'll let God inside your heart, where he can birth his plan for you. Hopefully you'll begin to recognize and respond to his call.

Learn who you are. Then start asking, *What's next?*

Fifteen or fifty-five, you are God's answer to somebody's questions. Take 21 days to launch a life of change—change in yourself, changing your world.

The journey's about to begin.

Any questions?

How to Use This Book

Welcome to 21 days of discovery. This book is your *Discovery Guide*. Over the next three weeks…

- You're going to take a close look at Jesus. Who is he…really? Is he powerful enough? Smart enough? Loving enough? Why do you need him?

- You're going to take a close look at yourself. Who are *you*? How did God specially design you? Are you valuable? Are you redeemable? What's your potential?

- And you're going consider your purpose in life. What's your mission from God? Will you like it? How will God make sure you can fulfill it? What can you expect along the way?

The Pray21 journey is a team event. Young people and adults, in pairs or groups, should think, talk, and pray together through these 21 days. All ages are vital to victory.

The apostle Paul wrote to a young pastor in 1 Timothy 4:12: "Don't let anyone put you down because you're young. Teach believers with your life: by word, by demeanor, by love, by faith, by integrity." Most of Jesus' disciples were teens and twenty-somethings when he left them on their own to continue his mission—with his Spirit to guide and strengthen them.

God has always counted on young people to do great things for him. He still does.

But this growth opportunity isn't just for the young. *Everyone* has to take it personally. No aloof supervisors—just participants, fellow pilgrims. We urge humility, respect, and honesty from all ages. Encouragement and accountability must flow both up and down the age scale. None of us has arrived; all of us need to learn from each other.

Each of the 21 daily readings is guided by a question that Jesus asked. His questions were among his best tools for cutting to the heart of people's real issues. Listen carefully as he asks you these questions.

The daily stories—from the Bible, from history, from famous and unknown people today—help illustrate and answer Jesus' questions. We've added a few questions of our own ("Brief Debrief"). Each day's questions are also included in the separate *Pray21 Journal*, with extra space for your written responses, plus your other thoughts, commitments, and prayers. Private journaling is especially important for the days you read on your own, between meetings with your partners. Bring your most important questions, insights, and commitments to share when you connect with your group.

Each reading offers a suggested prayer ("Secure Channel") for you to use or adapt, and Bible passages ("Background Files") to read for deeper answers to Jesus' questions.

Each day, you'll be challenged to choose one specific application for real life. But you can't possibly make 21 life changes in 21 days. So use the three weekly "Checkpoints" to narrow down to three commitments that especially stand out to you.

Spiritual discovery means eyes, ears, and heart open.

Open to a deeper relationship with your best Friend ever.

Open to forgiveness and healing, learning and growth.

Open to dreaming God's dream.

Open to doing more than you ever thought possible for him.

So much to discover…

PART 1:
BELIEVE

You believe in God? Good. Did you know that God believes in you?

God made you just the way he wanted you to be. Sure, maybe you've done things that have offended him, hurt others, and injured yourself. Not good. But that doesn't change the fact that God made you for himself (he really likes you) and for a purpose, a mission in this life. And he believes you can do it…with his help…because he made you that way.

So when does your purpose for living kick in? When do you get to start doing something really important? Will it be when you "grow up"? When you get a degree? When you get married? When you make partner or manager?

None of the above. Your purpose takes effect NOW! It doesn't matter whether you're a teen or an octogenarian. You've already passed Go. You've already collected all the gifting and spiritual resources from God that you need for mission launch. What? You don't have everything you'll need for the whole journey? Don't worry. God will train and supply you on the job. It's part of the "daily bread" Jesus said to pray for in Matthew 6:11.

But the whole venture starts by agreeing with God. He believes in the *you* that he made. You need to believe in that same you. Not with sinful pride, but with faith in your Creator and Provider as you step out and live for him.

So tell God, "You're right about me." And don't just tell him. Show him.

how many loaves do you have?

Scene 1

"Well done, Phil, my friend." The respect in Jesus' eyes and tone made Philip forget all about his tired muscles and sore feet.

Jesus moved on to the next disciple. Philip experienced total physical recall.

He collapsed against a nearby wall and slid to the ground. Jesus had sent the disciples out in pairs for weeks, preaching the kingdom and performing miracles village to village.

It was the most terrifying experience in Philip's life. He wouldn't have missed it for all the camels in Egypt.

"Okay, guys, listen up." Jesus waited until he had the exhausted men's attention. "You all deserve a break." He paused for effect. "How about a two-day retreat on the other side of Lake Galilee?"

Suddenly everyone scrambled like squirrels, searching for the nearest boat to rent. Philip had never seen Jesus laugh so hard.

They headed across the lake, thinking they had gotten away incognito. But as the supposedly isolated opposite shore came into view, the disciples groaned in unison. The beach was packed with people waiting for Jesus. The boat's occupants were very, very cognito.

"Sheep," Jesus muttered, scanning the crowd. "They're sheep. With no shepherd." Philip could almost feel the heartache waves emanating from Jesus. The day's work wasn't over.

Desperate people don't tend to think ahead. Several hours later, Philip pulled Jesus and a few of the disciples aside. "Lord, these people are starving. Why don't you send them away to find dinner?" *And to give us a break*, Philip didn't say.

Jesus seemed baffled. "What do you mean, Philip? You're an adult—a full fifteen years old. Why can't you feed them?"

It had to be the heat, finally getting to Jesus. Philip suppressed a scream and said with forced calm, "Well, we could do that…if one of us can just go work for eight months and earn enough to buy the bread!" He pictured himself returning months later with the grocery bags, thousands of skeletons littering the lake shore.

Jesus smiled patiently. "How many loaves do you have?"

That's when Andrew piped up. "Five, Lord. And two fish." He pointed to a boy holding a small parcel.

Jesus' eyes widened. "Good job, Andy!" Jesus slapped him on the shoulder. "Now have everyone sit down to eat."

When this was done, Jesus stood holding a few dinner rolls and a couple of mackerels. He thanked God for his provision. Then he added more quietly, "Thank you, too, Father, for men with the resourcefulness to bring everything they have to you."

An hour later, five thousand men, plus women and children, lounged on the grass fully satisfied, many napping. Philip helped load twelve baskets of leftovers into the boat.[1]

Scene 2 (four years later)

Jesus died, rose, and returned to heaven, leaving twelve men—mostly teenagers and twenty-somethings—in charge of God's world mission. But Jesus promised always to be with them, and proved it as the Twelve helped thousands more become Christ-followers in Jerusalem.

Among those thousands was, of course, another Philip. They called him "Greek Phil," after his mother tongue, to distinguish him from our friend, "Hebrew Phil." Almost exactly the same age, the two became best friends and spent whole days talking about everything Jesus—including the Lesson of the Loaves that had so impressed Hebrew Phil.

Then on short notice, Greek Phil had to relocate. Now he was feeling like a poodle in a pigsty. In downtown Depravity Central…

Samaria. Land of the traitorous half-breeds. Any Jewish blood in their veins was centuries ago contaminated with that of the idolatrous heathen. Samaria was a cultural cancer festering in the middle of Israel.

"At least I ditched those Jerusalem temple goons," Philip muttered.

That rabid Pharisee, Saul, had stirred up persecution against Jesus' followers. Thousands fled Jerusalem, and Philip ended up…here.

Time to get started, Philip. There was no mistaking the Lord's voice. *The mission continues here.*

Philip started to hyperventilate. He glanced frantically around at the people. No, the *animals.* He wanted to run to someplace clean.

"Lord, you can do anything. But with me? Are you saying that I have enough…loaves…for *this*?"

That's exactly what I'm saying. Just give me everything you have.

So, shaking in his sandals, Philip proceeded to preach the message of the Messiah. And his heart changed. He touched the sick and crippled; they were healed. He commanded demons; they fled. And, greatest of all miracles, the Samaritans believed in Jesus! By hundreds. By thousands.

Peter and John came from Jerusalem in person to see what their ears couldn't believe. They left convinced.

That's when God said, *Philip, time for your next assignment. Travel south.*

Scene 3 (three days later)

A long, hot road. Chariot approaching. A beauty! Two horsepower. Iron rims. Upholstered seats. Ethiopian make. Last year's model, no less! Someone with power. And money.

The chariot rolled past, a servant driving and a lavishly dressed, dark-skinned official sitting, reading a scroll.

Keep up with them.

Philip swallowed hard. "If you say so, Lord." He ran to catch up, then jogged alongside.

When Philip heard the official reading aloud the words of Scripture, he struck up a conversation. Soon he found himself sitting in the chariot beside—get this—the royal treasurer of Queen Candice of Ethiopia! The Jewish faith fascinated the man, but he wasn't getting the Scriptures' meaning. So, riding in style, Philip found confidence to explain God's Word and its fulfillment in Jesus.

When they came to a stream, the Ethiopian pointed and said, "I want to be baptized into the Messiah. Right now!" Philip obliged.

He was helping the dripping, laughing man rise from the water when… everything faded. The stream. The Ethiopian. Vanished! Five seconds later a different scene materialized around Philip—a seacoast town.

Teleportation! Just like his other brother Phil said he saw Jesus do after his resurrection! That day in the locked room, Jesus just popped into the middle of them and started talking.

Philip scanned his new surroundings. *It figures*, he thought. *No one here to see.*

Scene 4 (five days later)

And so, starting in that town, Ashdod, Philip preached from village to village up the Mediterranean coast, spreading the good news of Jesus.

Now he was resting by the dusty road, hours away from his next stop. He squinted up at the glaring sun. In spite of his cracked lips and the sweat dripping off him, he smiled. "Lord, you're amazing. With each new challenge, I bring you everything I have—a weary body, a forgetful mind, a willing heart—and you always multiply my few loaves into a feast for thousands." He knew Jesus was smiling back.

Time to get going. He rose, stretched, and stood looking north.

"Hey, Lord, it's hot. I'm shot. Couldn't you just beam me to that next village?"

Nothing happened. Philip heaved a sigh. And started walking.[2]

 ## Brief Debrief

Think through these questions. They're for everyone who follows Christ. Whether fifteen or forty-five, we all frequently need to recommit ourselves and our resources to him.

Dig deep and journal about them in your *Pray21 Journal*. Connect with others. Help each other process and pray through the questions and challenges. After you've arrived at some conclusions, continue praying for and supporting each other.

- What tempts you to think that you don't have what it takes to accomplish God's mission? What do you wish you could do for God and others, but are afraid to do? What thoughts and emotions do you wrestle with?

- How many loaves *do* you have? (Be honest.) How might God honor your small-seeming gift?

- What is he asking you to do for him or others this week? Why will this be of value?

- What will you bring to him, for his use?

- What support or resources do you need from others this week? What do they need from you?

Secure Channel

Lord, when I let myself dream, I get really pumped about all the things I'd like to do for you, and for people. For example…[go ahead, dream with God]…

But I'm usually afraid I don't have what it takes. I hear what you want from me, and I give up before I start. To be honest, I'm afraid you're unrealistic—that you want me to give what I don't even have.

But you promise that that's not true. You just want what I have…everything I have. And as small as that seems to me, here it is. Here I am. As an act of faith in you, this week I will…[commit to one simple, stretching act of obedience]…

I pray these things, too, for [name your partners], that they would courageously give you everything, and that you would provide confidence in your complete sufficiency through them.

Thanks for listening. Thanks for caring. Thanks for letting me serve you.

Background Files

To learn more about the true historic events described in this chapter, read John 6:1–17; Mark 6:7–13, 30–45; 8:1–10; Acts 8.

do you really believe I can do this?

Somewhere among the top hundred favorite verses in the Bible is Ephesians 3:20: "God can do anything...far more than you could ever imagine or guess or request in your wildest dreams!" We love this promise. So we dream. Then we say, "There, God, go for it. Do something even greater than that!"

And we wait.

Sometimes we wait a long time, because we forget to read the second half of the verse: "He does it...by working within us, his Spirit deeply and gently within us."

God's ready to go. Any time you are.

Wake Up

Jesus was leaving Jericho when two blind men started screaming after him, "Lord, have mercy on us!"

His reply? It might seem a little strange: "What do you want me to do for you?"[3] Wasn't it obvious? They were, like, *blind*, dude.

But Jesus knew what he was doing. He wanted more than information. He was inviting the men to participate in their own miracle, to voice their dream. When they did, he brought galaxy-creating power to bear.

That's what he'll do for you. If you'll dream with him. If you'll step into that dream and start living it out in his power.

He did this for Zach Hunter. Zach was an ordinary twelve-year-old when he started dreaming. (He's fifteen now, and he's still ordinary. Still dreaming.) But the extraordinary happened, because Zach followed a recipe that pureed three ingredients together: *information, passion,* and *an Almighty God.*

Information: During Black History Month, Zach discovered modern-day slavery. Today there are 27 million slaves in the world—more than during all four hundred years of the Trans-Atlantic African slave trade. Half of today's number are children, doing grueling labor under violent, abusive conditions; serving as sex slaves; some even in the United States. Slavery is the only existence many will ever know.

Passion: Inside Zach stirred a powerful sense of justice and compassion. *What if it were me?* he wondered. *Or my best friend, or my brother? Or my mom?* He pictured himself shackled all day, sitting on a dirt floor, forced to roll cigarettes. He imagined having a drug-addicted father who sold him into slavery to get his next high. He realized that right that second, millions were enduring that living death. People like him, who owned nothing—not even themselves.

It wasn't right. Something had to be done.

An Almighty God: God's kingdom grows in ways we can't explain by any natural means. Jesus likened it to a tiny seed that grows into a huge tree. Or a tiny pinch of yeast that eventually permeates a mass of dough, changing it drastically and visibly, by invisible means.[4]

Zach wanted to be the seed, one gram of yeast, and let God change the world through him. He dreamed. *I want to see modern slavery abolished worldwide in my lifetime.* And he launched his dream, starting the Loose Change to Loosen Chains campaign in his school, raising over eight thousand dollars to liberate slaves.

God had joined the mix.

In the three years since, Zach has joined forces with other like-minded people and organizations to educate, motivate, and activate people for the abolition of slavery. Zach speaks nationally. He's written a book entitled *Be the Change*, challenging his generation to make a difference. And he's the student spokesman for an antislavery initiative, The Amazing Change (www.amazingchange.com), inspired by the 2007 movie *Amazing Grace*.

"Working together, we can get a lot more done."

The movie depicts the life and passion of William Wilberforce, one of Zach's strongest role models. Wilberforce (1759–1833) lived in England at the height of the African slave trade. He was elected to Parliament at twenty-one, made a commitment to Christ at twenty-five, and soon began to lead a national effort to end slavery. After two decades of fighting, he finally passed a bill outlawing slave trading. And twenty-six years after that, a bill passed emancipating slaves throughout the British Empire—shortly after Wilberforce's death.

Look Up

Two other blind men. Different city. Different time. (Apparently they came in pairs.) They also begged loudly for Jesus' help. But this time he asked a different question: "Do you really believe I can do this?"[5] When they answered, "YES!" he said, "This is happening because you believed it could." And he gave them sight.

With the first blind men, Jesus was asking, Will you take yourself and your dreams seriously? This time he was asking, Will you take me, the dream fulfiller, seriously?

At times Zach's dream has faltered. When he started the Loose Change campaign, he suffered from a strong anxiety disorder. But God helped him overcome it. What might have paralyzed Zach at the nice-idea stage gave way before the God he believed in.

He faces other challenges, too. "Sometimes after I speak," he says, "a racially bigoted person will argue with me about slavery. They'll say I'm full of myself. That hurts, because I'm just trying to do what God has put on my heart. It can get me down.

"But every time, someone else comes up and asks, 'What can I do to help?' I think that's God's way of helping me put the discouragement behind me and move on."

Interdependence is a big theme for Zach. "To fulfill a dream, you have to work with other people. That can get messy, because people are different, especially when you're working with people from different generations. But with God's help we can set aside our petty differences. Working together, we can get a lot more done."

The Amazing Change website reminds us, "Wilberforce didn't abolish slavery by himself; he had a circle of friends and supporters to help him."

Zach's dream has come true because of the obedience of thousands of others. One girl signed over to the Loose Change fund two gift checks from her grandmother. Other kids have given their entire life savings to free slaves.

Where do others fit into your dream? Or you into theirs?

Ramp Up

Zach has another, broader dream. "I love to see young people like me giving themselves to something bigger than themselves. My dream for my generation is that we'd be the generation that really cares about the poor and changes things. That history books will say we were the peace, love, and justice generation, guided by Christ, dependent on him.

"I talk to young people about passion. When my generation's attention is drawn to something—a cause, a fad—they can get really excited. But that excitement doesn't last. We seem to be numbed against sustaining our passion. When MTV first started, students wouldn't let anyone take it away from them. But now it's just another channel—just more numbing noise.

"The enthusiasm has been drained from us. And it's because the enemy doesn't want us to be passionate about anything. Because that passion can be used for God. Like when Saul was persecuting Christians in the Bible, he did it wholeheartedly. But then God got hold of him, turned him around, and used that passion to take the gospel to the world."

We need the passion of William Wilberforce, who once said, "They charge me with fanaticism. If to be feelingly alive to the sufferings of my fellow-creatures is to be a fanatic, I am one of the most incurable fanatics ever permitted to be at large."

We're talking about a passion for God himself, which fuels a passion for everything he cares about. A passion that's not afraid to dream. A passion that gives yourself to the dream.

A passion that shouts "YES!" when Jesus asks, "Do you believe I can?"

BRIEF DEBRIEF

Dream about these questions, and write your thoughts in your *Pray21 Journal*. Think big with a big God (no matter your age or experience). Think and pray big with your partners. Plan together for action.

- "What do you want me to do for you?" What's your dream for God, for changing the world?

- "Do you really believe I can do this?" How big is your God? Big enough for your dream?

- If you haven't already, turn your dream into a request. Step up to the throne and petition the King to make it happen.

- What will be your first step in living the dream?

- Who else do you need to dream and live it with you?

SECURE CHANNEL

Lord, you asked for it. So here's my dream: [Spill it].

There. It's out. Now I choose to see you big, to believe that you can do what I've asked, and even more. Help me trust you, and trust that you made me right for your task. Fill me with true passion for you and your dream.

I pray for all of us [name your partners], that we'd encourage and support each other's dreams, that we'd learn to work in unity for your kingdom.

BACKGROUND FILES

To learn more about living God's dream, read Matthew 9:27–31; 20:29–34; Ephesians 3; Philippians 3:1–14.

do you believe in the Son?

Today we might call him Charlie or Chuck. But Charles grew up in England in the mid-1800s, when going to church was SOP (Socially Obligatory Protocol). Everyone did it, especially in cosmopolitan London.

Charles Spurgeon's father and grandfather were both pastors, and Charles spent his childhood years happily devouring theology books in their libraries. At seven he learned to read Latin, Greek, and Hebrew.

But although Charles was learning the Bible backward and forward, he was spiritually dead. He didn't know Jesus. He felt a growing misery he didn't understand.

One day the fifteen-year-old Charles attended a service where an inexperienced preacher taught the way to salvation through faith in Jesus. That's when Charles began an explosive relationship with Christ that would shake the world. His impact is still reverberating in millions of lives today.

A miracle life started with a miracle relationship.

Months later, Charles preached his first sermon. On short notice he proclaimed the preciousness of Jesus to a small group meeting in a cottage, moving his hearers deeply. His reputation spread, and he was soon in demand in pulpits around the countryside.

At seventeen, he became a pastor and spent two years growing his church from a mere handful to four hundred. Charles's love for Jesus was contagious, drawing and changing people who were tired of the plastic preaching in many churches.

He was nineteen when he started pastoring another church in seedy southern London. That congregation outgrew its building twice in four years. He preached in other locations, routinely to standing-room-only crowds of thousands. He once conducted a service in Glasgow where twenty thousand had to be turned away for lack of space.

He was twenty-six when work was completed on the Metropolitan

Tabernacle in London, seating six thousand. This would be home base for the rest of his life.

Sounds rosy, no? It wasn't. Charles stuck by his convictions in the face of any opposition. He spoke the truth, no matter who didn't like it. Even in his teens and twenties, while he was popular with many, he was very unpopular with powerful people representing the fossilized religious establishment. He preached against meaningless "faith" and cost-free "commitment." He preached a passionate love for Jesus and confronted the religion of the fashionable Messiah. This attracted oppressive, deeply discouraging criticism.

Newspapers were the only mass media then, and they held great sway over public opinion. The London papers united in their hostility toward Spurgeon. Imagine trying to speak the truth to your city, only to have every TV and radio station, every newspaper, every magazine, and every website and blog turned against you. Your lone, small voice against a thousand megaphones. That's how Spurgeon felt as a minister barely two decades old.

But Charles knew Jesus. And that made the difference.

Knowing the Son always does.

Speaking of Jesus, there was a time when he came across a blind man. Born blind. We'll call him Phred. Jesus did a trick with spit and dirt and—don't try this at home—put the mud on the blind man's eyes. He told him to go wash it off. (Duh.)

After Phred did this, he could see!

Of course he made a big deal about it. That attracted the Phrightening Pharisees—the phossilized religious leaders—who started questioning him.

You can become a brand new person just by asking.

"Who would dare make mud and heal on the Sabbath? Work...on the holy day of rest?"

"It was Jesus," said Phred.

"Well, Jesus is a sinner. And we don't believe you were blind."

They found his parents, who were phrightened of the Pharisees and said, "Yep, he's our boy. And he was blind. But we don't know anything. Ask him."

By now Phred was getting phed up. "I'm telling you what I know. I was blind, now I see. Why do you ask? So you can become Jesus' disciples?"

The Pharisees phairly phoamed at the mouth. "This Jesus is a nobody. We don't even know where he's from."

Phred rolled his brand new eyes. "He's from God, idiots!"

They called him a sinner and made him go away.

Jesus heard of this, and when he found his patient, he asked, "Do you believe in the Son of Man?" ("Son of Man" was one of Jesus' favorite ways of talking about himself.)

Phred begged, "Please, show me who he is. I want to believe in him."

Jesus smiled. "Don't you recognize my voice?"

"It's you! Oh, yes, Lord, I believe!" And he dropped to the ground and worshiped.

Phred needed more than eyesight. He needed to know the Son.

A miracle relationship initiated a miracle life.[6]

Knowing the Son, Charles Spurgeon's life became a spiritual vortex. Knowing Jesus, he pressed forward when the world opposed him. He almost gave up, but he kept confronting the convenient "Jesus" and the soft "faith" of pseudoChristianity. Some of his most intense battles were near the end of his life. In spite of debilitating health problems, Charles preached truth while his body endured. His Jesus sustained him in a history-shifting cause. He took his last breath at age fifty-seven, eight months after his last sermon at the Tabernacle.

Now he knows the Son even better.

Do you know the Son? Your parents might be Christians. You may have gone to church for a year. Or eighty. None of that matters. If you don't know Jesus personally, you're still not a child of God.

You can be sure. Now. Your sins separate you from God and deserve eternal punishment. Jesus died in your place to pay for your sins. Once you accept the free gift of his sacrifice, God sees and judges you the way he sees Jesus—free from condemnation. He also changes you inside, so you're able to start conquering the sins that have trapped you.

You can become a brand new person just by asking. You can pray the prayer below (see "Secure Channel"), but God sees your heart attitude, no matter what you say.

One hundred percent of the stock in every corporation on earth couldn't compare in value to your relationship with the Son. Spurgeon, when he was twenty, once preached about the worldwide implications if the Name of Jesus were removed from earth. At one point he burst out, "I would have no wish to be here without my Lord; and if the gospel weren't true, I'd thank God to annihilate me this instant. I wouldn't want to live if you could destroy the name of Jesus Christ."[7]

Years later his wife remembered that event:

I honestly thought he might die there, in front of all those people!… He could hardly speak, and only through fragmented speech could his feeble closing be heard: "Let my name perish, but let Christ's Name last forever! Jesus! *Jesus!* Jesus! Crown Him Lord of all! You will not hear me say anything else." …And then he fell back almost fainting in the chair behind him.

The miracle life starts with a miracle relationship.

BRIEF DEBRIEF

Think about these questions, talk with God about them, and journal in your *Pray21 Journal*. When you meet with others, share your thoughts and feelings honestly. Pray together for true knowledge of Jesus, no matter how old you are, and do what you can to help each other find him.

- What's the difference between knowing Jesus and knowing *about* him?

- What's the difference between knowing Jesus and doing the good things he says to do?

- If someone asked you how to start a relationship with Jesus, what would you say?

- Do you know the Son of Man? You can pray to him now, using the following prayer or any words that convey the same ideas. Then you'll have his presence in you, helping you live the life you've always really wanted.

SECURE CHANNEL

Jesus, I've done wrong things, and I don't deserve forgiveness or heaven. Thank you for dying for me. I accept your forgiveness, your free gift of eternal life. Change me inside, and help me live for you. Thank you for this miracle *in* me. Now do miracles *through* me.

And if you know Jesus... Lord, thank you for being in my life. Never let me take you for granted. Pull [name your partners] and me closer to you. Let us actually feel like we're starving when we neglect you, so we'll seek you with all our hearts. Live through us and change our world.

BACKGROUND FILES

To learn more about starting a relationship with the Son, read John 9:1–41; 1 John 5:11–15; Romans 3:20–25; Ephesians 2:1–10.

why did you doubt?

Peter couldn't *buy* a break. He was cold and tired. His back ached from rowing. The disciples had been fighting a vicious wind for hours, but their boat was making no headway. The night was closer to dawn than dusk, pitch black. Were they even heading in the right direction?

Jesus saw this coming. Peter sneered. *That's why he stayed behind.* Nothing in this day was going right.

First the disciples had come back from weeks traipsing around the countryside, preaching and performing miracles. Exhausted. Jesus took them across Lake Galilee for a restful retreat, only to find thousands of people waiting. And of course Jesus had to help them. Then the whole starvation problem came up.

Well, Peter thought, *I guess it was cool, the thing Jesus did with the food, feeding five thousand men and their families from one kid's lunch bag.* He stopped rowing and looked sorrowfully at the baskets of leftover bread, now soaked with lake water. At least the fish was okay.

His fatigued mind wandered. He recalled an especially affirming moment from the day, when Jesus had prayed over the bread and fish and added, "Thank you, Father, for men with the resourcefulness to bring everything they have to you." It was Andy and Philip who'd found the food. But Peter knew the Lord valued them all. Besides, Peter would have been the one to solve the problem…if he hadn't needed that nap so badly.

He was about to resume rowing, when he squinted into the dark. Was something out there behind them? There it was again! Coming toward them. Not another boat… It was…

"Ghost!" Peter shouted hoarsely, jumping up, bashing his heavy oar handle into Nathaniel's back. Everyone looked where Peter pointed. (Except Nathaniel—he was writhing on the boat's floor, holding his back and gasping for breath.)

Within seconds all were frantically shouting. "Turn to port!" "No, starboard!" "Hide me!" The ghost was coming right for them!

Then a familiar voice over the wind: "Calm down, you guys. It's just me."

It—it looked like… But so hard to see.

"Lord," hollered Peter, "if that's you…" If that's you, what? Dry out our soggy bread? Show me your driver's license? Tell Nathaniel to get up and stop being a baby? "If it's you, tell me to come out there with you."

He was barely able to make out an arm held out in a gesture of welcome. "Come on, Peter."

Peter had grown up in a boat, but still, large bodies of water had always intimidated him. All the campfire stories of what happened to drowning victims, the things that lived in the deep.

"It's the Lord," he muttered. "Do it." Without thinking, he climbed over the side.

And stood on a spongy, secure surface. Like really firm Jell-O. He looked down, bent his knees to absorb the up-push of a wave rolling under him. He looked up. Just in time to dodge the boat's bow, swinging at him. He saw Jesus twenty feet away, waiting.

Peter started quick baby-stepping toward Jesus. That's when he made his mistake. He started thinking again. Thoughts like, *If man were meant to walk on water, God would have made him with pontoons.* His feet felt wet.

He saw—shot of adrenaline!—that he was ankle-deep in the water.

Halfway to Jesus.

Waves towered over him, wind howled deafeningly. Peter took lunges toward Jesus. Water to his knees.

God has set this all up perfectly. This place. This time.

"Lord, save me!" he cried, as all support gave way. He sucked a quick breath. He was going to the bottom.

A strong hand grasped his wrist and held his upper body out of the water. Peter looked up and saw Jesus standing, looking sadly down at him. Not worried in the least, except about the example his second in command, Peter, was showing the others.

"So little faith," said Jesus quietly. "Why did you doubt me?"

The Lord's expression would stay with Peter longer than even the memory of his brief super-aquatic excursion. *I hate it when I let him down,* he berated himself as Jesus pushed him into the boat. Jesus climbed in, the wind died, and twelve men bowed and worshiped the true Son of God, King of heaven and earth.[8]

— — —

Several hundred years earlier, another figure bowed before a king. No linebacker-shaped fisherman, but a slender, beautiful teenage girl, dressed in the finery of a queen. Young wife of Xerxes, ruler of the Persian Empire, most powerful man in the world.

Her name was Esther. She was a Jew. And she was scared to death.

The next seconds would determine whether she would live or die. They might also mean extinction or survival for her people, Israel, scattered across the empire.

Esther still wasn't sure the fantasy-turned-nightmare was real. Her? A commoner, chosen to be queen of Persia? And then her Uncle Mordecai's discovery of the plot to wipe the Jews off the map.

Haman. She wanted to spit whenever she said that name. Arrogant, spiteful. Xerxes's most trusted adviser. Mordecai had refused to worship Haman—"No one but God," her uncle had said—and Haman had lost it. He found out Mordecai was Jewish, and conned Xerxes into signing a decree mandating the slaughter of the Jews throughout the empire on a chosen date.

The king had no clue. He'd just murdered his wife and everyone she loved.

But Uncle Mordecai was always thinking. "Esther," he said in a message, "you're the queen. Talk to the king, beg for mercy."

But it wasn't that simple. She wrote back, "It's common knowledge that anyone who comes into the king's presence without his invitation will be executed. Unless—but I've never heard of this actually happening—unless Xerxes holds out his golden scepter as a sign of pardon. I'd be walking to my death. It's been a month since Xerxes last called for me."

"Wake up, little girl," Mordecai replied. "The decree says *every* Jew must die. You think you can just lie low and survive? God has set this all up perfectly. This place. This time. This young lady. Do the right thing."

Esther sighed, and wrote back, "Tell everyone to fast and pray for me. I'm going in. If I die, I die."

It was a horrible weight for a teenager's shoulders. She needed help. And she found it in God's presence. Not freedom from fear, but the will to risk obedience in spite of fear. Doubt flooded her, and she kept pouring it into God's hands. Finally he helped her escape doubt's tyranny. Doubt became a choice, and she rejected it.

After three days she emerged and walked resolutely toward the throne room. She prayed outside the door, thought she might throw up, calmed herself, and walked into the king's view. She bowed her head in proper reverence, awaiting her fate. The fate of millions.

After counting the proper number of breaths, she prepared to raise her head. Then counted five more. She closed her eyes, stood straight. Then looked.

To see the gleam of the scepter. Held out toward her in her husband's strong hand. She could see in his face… Now he knew beyond any doubt the caliber of woman he'd chosen. He was smiling.

Because of a teenager's courage, her people—God's people—were saved. Haman hung from the gallows he'd built for Mordecai. And a young woman became a legend.[9]

Got doubts? Jesus understands. But he also wants to help you beat them. Unyielding skepticism becomes a smokescreen hiding our unwillingness to trust God, to take an obedient risk, to do the right thing. Jesus sees through it. So do you.

Got Jesus? Much better.

BRIEF DEBRIEF

Another day, a bigger challenge. Don't face it alone. Connect with your partners soon, and share encouragement, accountability, and prayers. Connect with God about these questions, and write your responses in your *Pray21 Journal.*

- Describe one doubt that makes it hard for you to trust and obey God.

- What helps you beat it? What makes it worse?

- How do you need people? What can we do for you?

- Don't wait for fear to disappear. Fear isn't the opposite of faith. Disobedience is. What step will you take to show faith in spite of fear this week?

Secure Channel

Lord, it's hard to admit that I doubt you. I do. [Go ahead. Tell him how you doubt.]

Thanks for understanding. And thanks for not letting me stay stuck. Give me the will to obey, no matter how I feel. And when we've won a victory, let me feel your smile.

I know that [name your partners] are feeling doubts about [fill the blank]. Please give them courage, too.

Background Files

To learn more about dealing with doubt, read Matthew 14:22–33; Joshua 1:7–9; the book of Esther.

don't you know me yet?

If only I could see Jesus, talk with him, get to know him. If only I could go back in time, or have him show up here. Then it would be a lot easier to believe and to live the way he wants me to.

Have you ever thought something like that? One of those seeing-is-believing kinds of wishes.

Actually, the sentiment behind this wish is true—seeing Jesus is one of the most important ways to strengthen your faith. At least, it worked for Ruby.

Ruby Nell Bridges was born in 1954, the year that the US Supreme Court declared racial segregation in public schools unconstitutional. Throughout her first six years of life she knew nothing about the storm clouds that gathered across the nation, darkened, prepared to descend and let loose their fury on the front steps of a school building only blocks away from her New Orleans home.

Those six years of Ruby's life were focused on kid things. Playing with friends, attending kindergarten at an all-black school. Praying with her family and going to church every Sunday. Ruby learned early about the nearness of God at all times. She grew up seeing Jesus, her Friend.

One Sunday in the fall of first grade, her mother told her she would switch to a different school the next day.

The next morning, November 14, 1960, a car with four armed federal marshals drove Ruby and her mother the few blocks to the all-white William Frantz Public School. Ruby thought all the barricades and crowds were a Mardi Gras celebration. Many of the people were spitting, shouting horrible words, and throwing things. The marshals surrounded mother and daughter, two in front and two behind, as they walked from the car to the school's front doors. The arrangement reminded Ruby of God's protection before and behind her.[10] She saw Jesus, her Guardian.

That whole first day, Ruby and her mother sat in the principal's office while white parents dragged their children out of class, pointing angrily at the two black faces through the office windows.

On the second day, a smiling white woman named Barbara Henry met them, the only teacher willing to teach a black child. She took Ruby to her first-grade classroom. It was empty. No kids. Ruby thought she was there early. As it turned out, all the other kids were really, really late. Most of the school's five hundred-plus students wouldn't return until the next fall. Ruby was a class of one that year.

Mrs. Henry treated Ruby with kindness, and the two of them grew very close. Although Ruby missed learning, playing, or eating with friends, her loneliness was made tolerable by Mrs. Henry's love. In the person of her teacher, Ruby saw Jesus, her close Companion.

The third morning, Ruby's mother had to stay home with the younger kids. "The marshals will take good care of you, Ruby Nell," her mother assured her. "Remember, if you get afraid, say your prayers. You can pray to God anytime, anywhere. He will always hear you." And so she started daily praying on the ride to school, for herself and for the people who hated her so much. She prayed that God would forgive them, because they didn't know what they were doing. Just like Jesus prayed on the cross.[11]

She saw Jesus, the Forgiver, and wanted to be like him.

Through the winter she experienced nightmares. She'd run to her mother, who'd tell her to pray. She would return to her bed, kneel, and talk to her Friend. The fear always disappeared. She met with Jesus, her Comforter.

Because of the national attention, Ruby's father was fired from his job as a service station attendant. And the family was refused service at a local grocery store. But people from across the country sent encouraging letters and donations. A neighbor gave her father a job painting houses. Friends helped with babysitting and watching the house for trouble. Ruby saw Jesus, her Provider.

Any time with Jesus is time to get to know him.

Once second grade started, things got back to normal at Ruby's new school. Except that Mrs. Henry wasn't there. She'd been uninvited from teaching. Ruby completed her years at William Frantz, then graduated from high school. She became a travel agent, then married Malcolm Hall and began the hard work of raising four boys.

When her brother died in 1993, she took in her three nieces, who attended…William Frantz Public School. Walking into that building was like reliving history. She began volunteering at the school where she'd made history thirty-plus earlier. She also established the Ruby Bridges Foundation, fighting racial injustice by teaching kids that everyone is valuable and important. She sees clearly the Jesus of justice and compassion, which gives her a passion to stop bigotry before it starts, in the minds and hearts of children.

If only we could all see Jesus. Hang around with him. Spend, say, a year or two or three learning from him.

Take a fresh look at him. Put up your Jesus antennae.

Well, that's what Jesus' twelve disciples got to do. And it didn't seem to give them any great advantage over Ruby. Philip had enjoyed the benefit of three years living and training with the Messiah when he said something that deeply disappointed Jesus. The details aren't important here. But Jesus' response is: "Don't you know me, Philip, even after you've been with me all this time?"[12]

What about you? How long have you been with Jesus? A month? A decade? Fifty years? Any time with Jesus is time to get to know him. In person.

You can see him. He's speaking to you every time you read or hear or remember something from the Bible. It's his Spirit who whispers (or shouts) to your conscience, giving you courage and clarity in life's fog. It's his conviction you feel when you get mad about something that's wrong. His love, when you feel compassion for someone who's hurting. You see him in the answers to your prayers; even if the answer is no, or something you didn't expect, that's him, teaching you. Whenever one of your brothers or sisters in Christ does something kind, or lovingly corrects you, or prays for you…that's Jesus, hugging you with his "body," the church.

You can even see him when you pass a homeless person, observe a fatherless child, or watch a jailed criminal's face on TV.[13]

After all your time with Jesus, how well do you know him? He's been there.

Take a fresh look at him. Put up your Jesus antennae. Open your ears. Sensitize your heart. See him?

Ruby saw Jesus with a child's wide-open eyes from the earliest possible age. So by the time she needed him most, she knew him well enough to brave challenges that would take many of us down. She knew he was safer than a federal marshal, stronger than a mob, more forgiving than human hatred, and more comforting than her own mother. He would see her through anything, because she saw him.

And so she changed the world.

Looking back, Ruby's mother summed up the historic impact of her daughter's faith: "Our Ruby taught us all a lot. She became someone who helped change the country. She was a part of history, just like generals and presidents are part of history. They are leaders, and so was Ruby. She led us away from hate, and she led us nearer to knowing each other, the white folks and the black folks."[14]

How will *your* fresh vision of Jesus change *your* world?

BRIEF DEBRIEF

As you dig into and journal about these questions, picture Jesus there conversing with you. (He really is.) Absorb the love, power, and truth of his Presence. Renew your commitment to seek him each day. Share your commitment with your partners, and prayerfully support each other.

- What are some ways you've seen and come to know Jesus personally in your time with him?

- What difference has this vision of him made in your attitudes and way of living?

- In what ways do you need to open your eyes to Jesus, take a fresh look at him, revive your relationship with him?

- What's one step you'll take now to see and know Jesus better?

SECURE CHANNEL

Jesus, I want to see you. I want the fulfillment of a deep friendship with the God of everything, the central character of all human history. You.

I know I've disappointed you at times, neglecting you, running from you, pretending to be your friend when I've been more like a stranger to you. I'm sorry.

Give me hunger to know you through your Word and prayer. And give me awareness to see your hand and heart in people and events around me.

I pray for the same hunger and sensitivity in my friends, [name your partners].

BACKGROUND FILES

To learn more about seeing and knowing Jesus better, read Matthew 25:31–46; John 14:1–18; 15:1–17; Acts 4:13.

PART 2:

BELONG

An amateur once challenged a golf pro to a round…on one condition. The amateur requested two "gotchas." The pro wouldn't admit he didn't know what a gotcha was, so he said okay. The amateur's opening drive was horrible, sliced into a thick grove of trees. The pro teed up, eyed the fairway, and drew back. That's when the amateur dug him in the ribs and yelled, "GOTCHA!"

Later, the other golfers learned that the amateur had won by five strokes. When they asked the pro, all he said was, "You have no idea what it's like playing eighteen holes, waiting for a second gotcha."

We all have gotchas in our past, no matter how long that past is. Trauma, family wounds, painful relationships, sin, failures, labels. We live with ongoing insecurity, waiting for our gotchas to jump up at any moment. They can hinder our relationship with God and our ability to serve him.

If you're a Christ-follower, you confront your gotchas by learning that you *belong*. You were chosen by God to be his forever, and to be part of his mission. You have a secure home waiting in heaven and a church family on earth. You're completely forgiven and accepted. And Jesus is with you through everything.

In these next days, you'll grow more confident in your belonging. But don't wait to launch into your God-given dreams and purpose. He'll use you now!

haven't I
handpicked you?

Crazy Horse. Soft-spoken, dedicated Lakota Sioux leader who fought to protect his people's way of life, he was revered as a hero long before his legendary victory over Custer and the US Seventh Cavalry.

George Washington Carver. Born into slavery during the Civil War, he battled his way to an education and eventually became a top chemist, inventor, and educator, preparing the way for minority success stories to follow.

John Hancock. Successful businessman, nine-term Massachusetts governor, and president of the Continental Congress, his bold signature on the Declaration of Independence is a national icon representing freedom and truth.

What do these three men have in common? Lots of things. They all stood by their convictions, even in the face of overwhelming odds. They all moved through life with confidence and courage. They were (and are) all held in high esteem for their moral character.

And they were all adopted. Loved…on purpose.

When Hancock was seven, his father died and his childless Uncle Thomas adopted him, cared for him as his son, and ensured him the best education. Hancock graduated from Harvard at seventeen and became a trusted partner in his uncle's business. Uncle Thomas left his entire estate to John when he died, making John the wealthiest man in New England at the time. Thomas loved John…voluntarily…and built strength of character into his nephew. So John Hancock devoted his life and fortune to support the American Revolution.

Several decades later, a teenage Sioux was adopted by a warrior named High Backbone. Loved…by choice. The boy, Crazy Horse, exercised a lifetime loyalty to his new father. Out of this close relationship grew a young leader who possessed, not only strategic military genius, but also quiet humility, sacrificial conviction, and deep compassion. He was reluctant to push back against encroaching settlers and resisted boasting about his successes. A six-hundred-foot-tall monument in his honor is partially completed, not far from Mount Rushmore in South Dakota.

Crazy Horse was twenty-four when, just a couple states to the southeast, a female slave was kidnapped by slave raiders. She was sold off before her owner, Moses Carver, could find her. Her infant son, George, had also been taken, and now was dying of whooping cough, "worthless" in the eyes of most slave owners and traders. But Moses ransomed George at great cost, and he and his wife, Sue, adopted George as their son. They loved him… consciously, willingly. The Carvers tried to give George an education in the white Missouri schools, but failed. So George, equipped with strong moral fiber by his adoptive parents, left home at ten and found his own education in various locations, eventually becoming the first African American to graduate from Iowa State College of Agriculture.

Three boys. All dearly loved. Loved on purpose. Three individuals out of billions.

"Even before he made the world, God loved us."

Of the six billion people who inhabit this earth, some are cherished by their earthly parents; some are not. But all share one incredible reality. A fatherly Creator in heaven crafted every—*every*—individual uniquely, each person reflecting God's amazing image in her or his singular way. God loves and treasures each one-of-a-kind child and adult. *On purpose.* He always has.

Jesus said, "God loved the world so much that he gave his one and only Son."[15] (Add about a million exclamation points after that.)

The apostle Paul wrote, "Even before he made the world, God loved us."[16]

King David sang,

Oh yes, you shaped me first inside, then out; you formed me in my mother's womb. I thank you, High God—you're breathtaking! Body and soul, I am marvelously made! I worship in adoration—what a creation! You know me inside and out, you know every bone in my body; you know exactly how I was made, bit by bit, how I was sculpted from nothing into something. Like an open book, you watched me grow from conception to birth; all the stages of my life were spread out before you, the days of my life all prepared before I'd even lived one day.[17]

Uncle Thomas, Moses and Sue Carver, High Backbone—all of these parents loved their boys voluntarily and sacrificially. Now try to imagine that kind of love coming from God…multiplied by infinity. God loved his Son, Jesus, far more than any human has loved a child. Yet he sent Jesus to experience misunderstanding and grief, pain and death, in his desire to rescue and adopt us for himself. That's God's on-purpose love for us.

Jesus said, "What is the price of two sparrows—one copper coin? But not a single sparrow can fall to the ground without your Father knowing it. And the very hairs on your head are all numbered. So don't be afraid; you are more valuable to God than a whole flock of sparrows."[18]

You are loved. You are valued. Just the way you are.

Believe it.

— — —

You've also been carefully chosen and crafted for a specific calling in your life.

During a discouraging time in the ministry of Jesus and his disciples, he reassured them, "Haven't I handpicked you, the Twelve?"[19] It helps to know you've been chosen on purpose, not just by default.

Jesus wants you! First for your friendship. (He likes you.) But also because you're valuable as a specialist-on-assignment, intended to carry out a preplanned, you-designed, you-customized, you-nique task in his mission.

That's why Jesus handpicked his men. Think, for example, of Matthew. Why would Jesus choose him? The man was scum. He worked for the Roman oppressors, collecting taxes from his own people. That's bad enough, but as was common practice among first-century IRS agents, Matthew charged extra "taxes" that never made it to Rome. Padding his pockets left many Jewish families destitute. He was a traitor and a thief.

But Jesus saw a heart that could be rescued, and a life that would fulfill a strategic assignment. Matthew was a record keeper, and his collected quotations and stories from Jesus' ministry comprise the book bearing his name in our Bibles today. Matthew had also been an astute observer of the Old Testament in his childhood education. In writing Jesus' story, he pointed out dozens of ways that the Messiah fulfilled Old Testament prophecies, reassuring Christ-followers throughout the centuries that Jesus is who he claimed to be.

Thousands of stories—in the Bible, throughout history, and in our world today—show handpicked children of God accomplishing often surprising feats as part of God's mission.

God made you with love. He paid his Son for your adoption as his own child. And he crafted you to fulfill a unique purpose on earth.

Maybe you'll protect the helpless.

Maybe you'll invent a lifesaving use for the peanut.

Maybe you'll stand up for truth.

Whatever your assignment, knowing that you're handpicked makes all the difference.

BRIEF DEBRIEF

Write in your *Pray21 Journal* about these questions, continually asking your Father to let you see yourself through his eyes. When you connect with your partners, be God's eyes and voice of love for them, too. Age is not an issue. Everyone needs reassurance.

- What do you honestly believe about your worth to God and your special design for his mission? What are you *told* is true about you, but have a hard time believing?

- What can you do to become more convinced of your value to God?

- What can you do to become more convinced that Jesus wants you on his team, that he has an important job for you to do?

- For today, don't work hard at figuring out what your life assignment is. Focus on simply believing it exists. What's one step you will take toward firmly grasping the truth of your value and purpose?

Secure Channel

Lord, forgive me for the times I insult you, believing you didn't make me right. Or doubting the power of your grace to clean me up. Or making too little of your amazing love for me.

I go back and forth between thinking too much of myself and thinking too little. (Maybe they're really the same.) Thank you for telling me exactly how you think and feel about me, not leaving me in the dark. Help me believe it. Let it fuel my confident obedience.

Please also show [name your partners] more of your love and your purpose for them. How can I help you answer this prayer in their lives?

Background Files

To learn more about your value and purpose in God's eyes, read Psalm 139; Matthew 10:29–31; John 3:16–18; Ephesians 1:3–14; 1 Corinthians 12:4–31.

what good to gain the world and lose your soul?

Message from Jesus, AD 30:
"Trust me. There is plenty of room for you in my Father's home. If that weren't so, would I have told you that I'm on my way to get a room ready for you? And if I'm on my way to get your room ready, I'll come back and get you so you can live where I live."[20]

Letter from Rosa, AD 1999:
I was born into a Communist home where no one could even mention the word God. I remember being a little girl looking at a huge picture of Fidel Castro (the leader of the Cuban Revolution) in my living room.

"If the world hates you, remember that it hated me first. The world would love you as one of its own if you belonged to it, but you are no longer part of the world.... They have rejected the One who sent me."[21]

My parents are atheists. My father used to be a representative of a very important organization called the Communists Youth Union. Now he is in the Cuban Communist Party leadership. My mother is secretary of the Revolution Defense Committee. In summary, my home is a Communist "nest."

"In this godless world you will continue to experience difficulties. But take heart! I've conquered the world."[22]

However, my great-grandmother loves God and she has been faithful to God through all these years. She used to talk to me about the Lord and she sowed the seeds of the Lord's Word. On several occasions I tried to go to church with her, but my parents did not allow me to go.

"The Son of Man is going to come in his Father's glory with his angels, and then he will reward each person according to what he has done."[23]

Years later my parents divorced, and then my mother allowed me to go to church, without my father's permission. Anyway, when I was twelve my mother tried to get me away from the Lord, organizing and inviting me to parties. I went away from the Lord living that way. But my great-grandmother persevered in praying for me.

"If you try to hang on to your life, you will lose it. But if you give up your life for my sake and for the sake of the Good News, you will save it."[24]

One day I went to church and received the Lord Jesus Christ as my Savior. My life started to change; even my way of dress changed totally. My mother did not accept it. She never beat me before, but now she does often.

"I am the way, the truth, and the life. No one can come to the Father except through me."[25]

When my father learned that I was a Christian, he told me to choose God or him. I chose the Lord because I have understood that He is the only thing really worthy for me. I know that God is faithful and He cares for me and He is going to do wonderful things for my family.

"Everyone who acknowledges me publicly here on earth, I will also acknowledge before my Father in heaven.... If you refuse to take up your cross and follow me, you are not worthy of being mine."[26]

My mother got married again to another Communist man. He had a five-year-old son. They don't allow me to talk to him about the Lord or go to church, but I talk to him about the love of God anyway. Sometimes I listen to him praising the Lord.

"Who do you think my mother and brothers are?... Obedience is thicker than blood. The person who obeys my heavenly Father's will is my brother and sister and mother."[27]

Now, even though I am only fourteen, I study far away from my home. When I first came to this place I was the only Christian, but I have sown God's Word and now we are four. We meet under a tree, hidden, to share God's Word. We feel the presence of the Lord in such a special way. We keep sowing and waiting that soon we will be many.

"Still other seeds fell on fertile soil, and they produced a crop that was thirty, sixty, and even a hundred times as much as had been planted!"[28]

God is faithful. He never forsakes His children. Please, pray for me. It is not easy to follow the Lord in a country so hostile to Him where opposition comes not only from the system but from our homes.

"Don't think I've come to make life cozy. I've come to cut—make a sharp knife-cut between son and father, daughter and mother, bride and mother-in-law—cut through these cozy domestic arrangements and free you for God."[29]

Our parents are blind in this atheistic system and do not understand that we grow and make our own personal decisions. Mine is Jesus Christ. I will be faithful even at the price of death.[30]

"If any of you wants to be my follower, you must turn from your selfish ways, take up your cross, and follow me.... What do you benefit if you gain the whole world but lose your own soul? Is anything worth more than your soul?"[31]

— — —

It's sometimes hard down here, because this isn't home. That's why, if you're actively following Christ, you're so often misunderstood.

Take heart.

We're strangers on earth, on a mission to rescue victims of the kingdom of darkness, and show them the way into the kingdom of the Son.[32] But some of the captives like the dark. So they shoot their rescuers. We get scared and stay home.

Turn out.

You may never face the threat of death for your faith. But the world system has a lot of ways of persuading Christians to give up. Don't take it lying down.

Stand up.

And no matter how your earthly family might treat you, in Christ you belong in an eternal family—God's family, the church. You were created with a built-in need to connect with other Christ-followers. Together we are able to worship God more powerfully, serve him as a unified body, reach out to the lost with a strong love, meet each other's needs, and support and challenge each other as we become like Jesus. Alone, you're duck soup.

Plug in.

BRIEF DEBRIEF

As you think and journal about these questions, call Home. Talk to your Father about them. And connect with your Homesick brothers and sisters, both older and younger. Talk and pray about this short earthly journey and the long eternity to follow.

- What are the things that tempt you to think of this world as home?

- Even with all the truly good things in this life, why is it dangerous to get too cozy down here?

- What are the possible risks of living as a child of Heaven? Why are they worthwhile?

- What's one new way you need to plug into God's family, your home away from Home?

- What is something on earth that your Father might be asking you to let go of, in order to stand up for him?

SECURE CHANNEL

Lord, thanks for all the gifts you've given me on earth, but help me get in touch with the unbelievably greater gifts in heaven—especially the ones I can have right now. You are the greatest Gift of them all.

To be honest, I think I'm too attached to [something on earth]. I've valued it more highly than you. Help me put things in the right order, you on top. And if that means giving something up, I will. Give me strength to do the right thing.

I pray the same for [name your partners]. Help us relate with each other as your family, helping each other through this earthly journey.

BACKGROUND FILES

To learn more about living on earth on the way to your heavenly Home, read Mark 8:34–38; John 14:1–6; 1 Peter 2:9–17.

one–week
checkpoint

Hey! You've just finished seven days of the Pray21 venture. How're you doing? Time to stop and take stock.

As we explained in the introduction, it's not humanly possible to actually do a new life application every day. In fact, the way God has designed us, a more realistic life growth pace is one new, deep, lasting life change a month. And that's someone who's really growing. (The way you want to grow, right?)

But these 21 days are different from normal life. They're your special gift to the Lord, meant as a focused time of seeking God's direction—a clarifying, foundation-building endeavor to launch the rest of your life serving him. So everyone participating in Pray21 is planning and praying for an especially concentrated dose of renewed devotion coming out of these three weeks—guided by one personalized commitment from each week.

You might come up with more than three ways you'd like to change, maybe dozens of promises you want to make and keep for the Lord. Write those down! Don't forget them. But for now, just narrow down to three— one each week—that you'll work on for the next couple of months or so.

Starting with this first week…

– – –

Think and pray about each of these checkpoint questions, and write your responses in your *Pray21 Journal*. Meet with your partners to talk and pray together about them, giving each other feedback and encouragement. Participants old and young should seek to learn from God and each other. As you consider this guidance and your own heart passions, choose one key commitment from Week One.

1. During the last seven days, what has been the most encouraging, uplifting thought you've had working through this *Discovery Guide*?

2. What has been the hardest idea or challenge for you to swallow? Why do you think this is so hard for you?

3. How have others been helpful to you as you've sought to learn and grow? What more could the rest of us do for you?

4. Have you been able to pray for, encourage, or lovingly challenge one or more of your partners toward growth? If so, describe one way you've done this.

5. Look back over your journaling for these first seven days. Think about the talks you've had with your partners. Does one challenge stand out as God's next step of growth and obedience for you? What is it?

6. **Rubber Meets the Road:** Write down a few details for following through on that next step. For example, what exactly will you do? When? Where? With whom? Who will support you and hold you accountable? How will you know when you've fulfilled your commitment? (Hint: Make your goal stretching and a little risky, but not unrealistic, so you don't just give up.)

7. From these first seven days, what other growth areas, goals, or commitments would you like to pursue some day? Write down a few of those dreams. You can come back to them later.

what's easier to fix— body or heart?

Jesus once told a paralyzed man, "I forgive your sins."

The religious skeptics grumbled, "Only God can forgive sins. Does he think he's God?"

God-in-flesh turned to them. He'd healed this man spiritually, mending the sin-rift between him and God. Now something visible was called for.

"Which is simpler," he asked, "to say 'I forgive your sins,' or to say 'Get up and start walking'?" No response. Jesus nodded. "Well, just so it's clear that I'm the Son of Man and authorized to do either, or both…"[33] He commanded the paralyzed man to go home. By foot. So the guy did.[34]

Jesus cares about our illnesses and injuries at every level. The spiritual wounds of sin that keep us from God. The physical maladies, which he sometimes heals, and sometimes, in his wisdom, leaves alone. And the emotional wounds of abandonment, abuse, loss, and more—which can hinder spiritual growth because they're closely tied to our ability to trust God, value ourselves, and make friendships.

Billy Buchanan of the Christian rock group Fusebox discovered God's multifaceted healing touch. Here's his story.

— — —

I watched from across the room as two of my guitar techs worked diligently to set up for my band's show. I'd noticed for a while that there was something different about the two guys. They seemed happier than most of the people I hung around, more at peace.

I wanted to know why.

When I had a chance, I decided to ask them.

"Why don't you guys party with us?" I asked. "How come you aren't interested in drinking and all the stuff the rest of us are into?"

One of the techs, Chris, looked me square in the eye.

"Man, God don't like it."

His answer stunned me. I'd expected a lot of things, but not to hear they were Christians. Now that he'd told me, it made sense. His statement reminded me there was a God out there I needed to serve, a God I'd grown up knowing but had quickly forgotten about.

Family Dysfunction

Life wasn't easy growing up. Many of my childhood memories involve abuse. I grew up in a dysfunctional home where music was my only escape.

My parents got married when they were young—my mom at seventeen, right after she graduated high school, and my father was only a year older. At eighteen, my mom gave birth to my brother, and I was born a year after that. By the time my mom was twenty-one, she had three kids.

My dad never really settled into the whole husband/daddy thing. I don't ever remember a time when he was content being a father or husband. He got into drugs and womanizing and all that stuff. That's how my dad was when I was growing up—it was all I knew.

My mom tolerated it for a while. When I was around ten, she got tired of being beat up all the time. She decided to leave my dad, and my parents got divorced.

Through all of that, my mom took us to church. I knew about the Lord. I knew about Jesus and what he did for me. But I didn't trust God very much, to be honest. The Bible told me that God loved and cared about me. But I questioned, if he did, then why did he allow my family to go through so much?

Rock-and-Roll Dreams

By the time I got out of high school, I was really into music. I had made up my mind to be a rock star. As soon as I graduated, I went to school in Cleveland, but then I dropped out and moved to Atlanta. While I went to school down there, I joined a band called Skindeep.

Within a couple of years, we were the biggest band on the Atlanta scene. We got really popular, really fast. By the time I was nineteen or twenty years old, we were playing for some really big crowds, opening up for acts like Alice in Chains, K.C. & the Sunshine Band, and Chaka Khan. I was living out my little rock-and-roll dream.

It's weird because my mom used to call me all the time and say, "Billy, are you going to church?" and I would just blatantly tell her that I wasn't interested. I was real anti-God at that point. I just didn't want anything to do with him.

But the conversation with the guitar tech had reminded me of the God my mother loved. The thoughts nagged at me, but I shoved them to the back of my mind. I was in a successful band. I couldn't let God destroy my dreams.

Empty and Tired

One night after a really big show of two or three thousand people, I came off the stage really empty and really tired of what I was doing. I came home and sat in my living room. I couldn't sleep and just stayed there until 3:00 or 4:00 in the morning, trying to figure out what was wrong with me.

I looked over at my bookshelf and saw the Bible. I knew that the answers were in that book. I opened it up. I can't remember exactly what I read, but I think it was in the book of John. Right then and there by myself, I got on my knees and said, "God, do something with me. I know I'm not being the guy that my mom raised me to be."

I came with all my baggage.

I woke up the next day and everything was different.

God's creation was more alive. I paid attention to the birds and the sky and the trees. It did take a lot of years for God to clean the junk that I was into out of my life. But life hasn't been the same since, that's for sure.

All My Baggage

I stayed in that band for probably another year or two after that experience. But when I started writing Christian songs, the band broke up. The songs started becoming more about my faith, and the guys in the band were like, "We don't want to get into this."

I got out of that band and took a year and a half off to rethink things. In that time, I became involved at a church and joined the worship team. I tried to get my head together and decide what God wanted to do with this talent he'd given me.

God's done a total transformation on me. I had the filthiest mouth of anyone you'd ever meet. I drank. I was with a lot of women. I did all of those things. When I became a Christian, all my friends told me, "Come as you are and God will change you, but don't think you have to change to come to God." I came with all my baggage.

I look back and really wish I hadn't gotten into this or that. I'm married now. I wish I would have waited to have sex. But I didn't. With any sin, you're going to reap what you sow. No matter what you were into before you were a Christian, there are definitely going to be consequences and results from that. But God is good, and his grace is sufficient. I know I don't have to dwell on any of those things anymore.[35]

Brief Debrief

God promises to forgive all sins when we ask him to.[36] He also heals emotional wounds with time.[37] Sometimes he heals our bodies, sometimes not.[38] Trust his compassion for you as you journal, pray, and connect with your partners.

- Do you have trouble believing in God's complete forgiveness and acceptance of you? If he's forgiven you, have you forgiven yourself, or sought forgiveness from others? Why might these steps be important?

- Is some physical or emotional injury keeping you stuck? If so, explain why. (See also Day 14.)

- Consider your fitness for God's mission. What one specific healing (of sin, emotions, or body) would you request?

- Once you've prayed for this, how can you step out in faith that the Healer has granted it, will grant it over time, or will enable you to live well even with this injury?

Secure Channel

Lord, I hurt. My spirit sometimes feels dirty. Help me stay close to you through confession, and give me confidence that you forgive and accept me completely. [Tell him specifics.]

You know best how and when to touch my other hurts. I give them all to you. [Tell him what they are.] Heal whatever I need in order to serve you best. Help me obey with patience and joy while enduring any injuries you don't heal, or that take time to heal. I'll be completely whole in heaven, but I can wait…and serve you…until then.

Also bring healing to [name your partners and specific requests for them].

Background Files

To learn more about Jesus the Healer, read Luke 5:1–32; 1 John 1:9; Hebrews 10:17–18; Isaiah 61:1–3; 2 Corinthians 12:7–10.

who loves God more?

Labels. They can be helpful. Like telling you the can contains a fusion of pseudomeat-filled pasta and pseudotomato sauce.

Labels can also hurt.

Idiot. Pervert. Loser. Addict. Ugly. Coward. Fat. Clumsy. Geek. Worthless. Thief.

A label on a can of food informs you. A label on a person enslaves you.

Let's follow the stories of two once-labeled women. One is named Becky Tirabassi, now a label-free speaker, author, and life coach. (We'll get to her later.) The other…well, we don't know her name.

But we can see her one day, two thousand years ago, cowering at Jesus' feet, frantically trying to escape the label she'd been trapped in for years…

Trash.

Her desperation gushed out in her tears—the tears she was crying onto Jesus' dirty feet. The salty grime she wiped from his feet with her hair was, to her, the filth that she felt smeared with.

Two men looked down on her. One was the dinner host, Simon the Pharisee, who saw only a label. "Prostitute!" he said in disgust.

Jesus saw a heart. His broke with hers.

He turned to Simon. "Mind if I tell you a story?"

"You're the teacher," said Simon.

"Once a rich guy made a couple of loans. He loaned one person fifty dollars, and another five hundred. Payback time arrived, and both debtors came up short. They had nothing. The rich guy was in a good mood, so he let them both off. 'Forget about it,' he said. 'Neither of you owes a dime.' And he wrote *forgiven* across their promissory notes.

"Which one do you think loved him more after that?"

"Well…" Simon saw where this was going. "I guess I'd have to say the one who had the bigger debt canceled. Although—"

"You're right," Jesus interrupted. He felt no obligation to be polite to someone who could treat another agonized soul so rudely. And he wouldn't let the Pharisee waffle on this issue. It was too important.

Jesus placed his hand on the woman's bowed head, his eyes watching her, but he spoke to Simon. "Yes, she has a truckload of sins. But they've been forgiven. Look how she shows her love." He glanced up. "I'm your guest, but you didn't offer me water to wash my feet, as is customary. She's washing my feet with her tears and drying them with her hair. You didn't greet me with the expected kiss on the cheek, but she hasn't stopped kissing my feet." Jesus shrugged. "But that's okay. Your sins must be microscopic, and so is your forgiveness. And your love."

He paused. Then he said to the woman, "Your sins are forgiven."

She gasped, still holding her face to his feet, then cried even harder—a death-row inmate just granted pardon. Awkwardly she rose. She flickered a moist, shy, grateful glance at her Savior. She left the house…label-free.[39]

Nineteen or twenty centuries later, another young woman struggled desperately to tear off her labels…

Failure. Liar. Lush.

Becky Jacobs was a teenage alcoholic.

She'd fought hard for popularity and acceptance. She didn't have looks, flashy clothes, or money. But she could make people laugh—especially when she was drunk. Alcohol became her game plan for fitting in. She became the life of the party.

Any party.

She worried a little when the blackouts started, leaving her with no memory of hours at a time. She started smoking. She experimented with drugs. She lied to her straight-laced parents; she smart-mouthed her teachers. When her heavy drinking came into the open, she declared an ongoing war with her mom.

To escape, she finished high school in three years. She tried college, work, boyfriends, running from the Midwest to California. Always looking for the next drink. Never finding happiness. Hating herself.

Curiously drawn to a California church building, she met a youth worker named Ralph. He spoke God's love and truth. But to Becky, her labels were her identity. Her essence. She didn't see any possibility of change.

When she was twenty-one, she was surprised to receive a summons for a formal court deposition. One night more than a year earlier, she had blacked out while driving drunk and crashed into a parked car. She lied and claimed that the other car had hit her. But the other owner was suing, and her sworn testimony was about to be recorded.

Becky had turned over many new leaves through the years, promising each time that she'd be different. Those leaves kept flipping back. By now she was deep in depression and self-loathing. She planned once again to start fresh. But this time it meant stopping the lies.

She almost lost her resolve to tell the truth about the accident, but God used a single word to get her attention. The man who prepared her for the deposition warned her, "If you lie and this case goes to trial, and they find out you lied, you will be *crucified* in court."

> God had saved her life... What's to be embarrassed about?

Crucified. She didn't hear anything he said next. Her mind flashed a picture of Jesus hanging on a cross. Ralph had explained to her what Jesus had done on her behalf. But this was the moment when God's Holy Spirit brought the truth home. She was struck with the purpose of Jesus' death. He died to redeem her messed-up life.

She endured the deposition, telling the truth throughout. Her next stop was to see Ralph at the church. With his help, she crouched at the feet of the Messiah and sobbed. He saw her heart, touched her bowed head, and canceled her entire debt. He welcomed the outcast, pardoned the condemned, dismissed the labels. And she walked out a free woman.

She knew that she was a new, truly different person. The change was so revolutionary to her that she told everyone who crossed her path. She never thought to be embarrassed. God had saved her life. Given her a *new* life! What's to be embarrassed about?

God relieved her of her craving for alcohol—as long as she didn't take a first drink. And soon she was free from drugs, telling the truth, reconciling with her parents, and running an unburdened race for Christ.

Within months she visited her old Chicago high school, to check in with some of the teachers and administrators whose existence she'd made so miserable. Through a series of divinely orchestrated "coincidences," she landed a job as a guidance counselor for teens using drugs and alcohol. Thus began her lifelong mission helping young people shed their labels and their old lives.

That was also the day she first spoke to the local Campus Life director, Roger Tirabassi. A few years later she became Becky Tirabassi, married now for twenty-nine years, with one son. Today she's a popular speaker and author of numerous books, including *The Burning Heart Contract*—a devotional that calls students to be sold out to prayer, set apart in purity, and set out with purpose. She is also founder of Burning Hearts Inc., a ministry designed to call today's young generation to live above the standards of culture (www.theburningheartcontract.com).

Only one label now wraps and enfolds Becky's life—a comprehensive blanket statement about her true essence and identity. She proudly claims the title, "Daughter of the King."

BRIEF DEBRIEF

These questions might challenge you to let go of something you've held dear for years—five years or fifty—something that's hindering you, or killing you. Think, pray, journal, and connect with others. You need help from God and people to release your cherished labels. And people need you.

- What labels do others put on you? Which labels are you most likely to let stick?

- Why do you believe them?

- Is there a difference between a sinful pattern of living and a label? If so, what's the difference? How do their solutions differ?

- If you haven't invited Jesus to forgive your sins, why not now? If you have, but you're still attached to an old label, how can you become convinced the label's a lie? (Truth: You're completely acceptable to your Father.)

- What's your first step?

SECURE CHANNEL

Lord, I've let something outside me define the inside-me. Something false. Something that fools me into thinking you can't love me.

Forgive me…for the sins, but also for the lies I believe about who I really am. I'm your child. I'm a new creation in Christ. I've been genuinely reborn, remade with a new heart. Help me believe it.

[Name your partners] also need to let go of their labels. Please help them experience your forgiveness and your complete acceptance.

BACKGROUND FILES

To learn more about Jesus' unconditional love for anyone with any label, read Luke 5:1–10; 7:36–50; Matthew 9:9–13; 1 Timothy 1:12–17.

what are you after?

"What? You saw him again today? Of all days for me to be gone." Andrew couldn't believe his timing.

He tried to spend as much time as possible with his teacher, John. ("John the Baptizer" he was popularly called. But he didn't like the nickname, so his disciples avoided saying it in his presence.) Andrew had been needed back home for a few days, to help with the family fishing business. He'd just this evening returned to John's semi-isolated ministry location, near the Jordan River's east bank. If he'd only come back a day earlier, he would have seen…the Messiah?

"Come with me tomorrow," replied John. "Maybe he'll be there again." John bit into a hunk of bread, tore off a mouthful, and started chewing noisily. He absently brushed his unruly hair out of his face.

Andrew smiled to himself. His teacher turned a lot of people off. In fact, when Andrew first responded to the rumors and came several weeks ago to hear John preach, he immediately wished he'd stayed home. Soon, however, John's unorthodox appearance and habits were forgotten, and his fiery proclamations took on the ring of solid truth.

This was no wacko. Colorful, yes. But he was also smart. He knew his Scriptures. And when he spoke of God and the Messiah, his face went all… rapturous (the best word Andrew could think of).

John waved his bread loaf at the handful of his disciples who reclined around the dinner table. "Can you believe people keep asking if I'm Elijah?" He shook his wooly head. "Or one of the other prophets. But what really bakes my bagel is when they think I'm the Messiah! Me!"

"Well, teacher," said Josiah, an older follower, "you can surely understand the mistake."

"No!" John shot to his feet. "I'm only the forerunner. Don't you dare confuse me with him. I'm not worthy to tie his sandals. My mission is to be the 'voice' Isaiah the prophet spoke of…calling out in the desert, 'Clear the way! The Lord is coming!'"

The disciples grinned at each other. He was on a roll now.

John gestured vigorously. "I baptize people with water, when they repent from sin. But the one who's coming, he'll bring a better baptism. He'll baptize people with God's Holy Spirit!"

He paused for effect—an opening Andrew jumped into. "Teacher, you're certain he's the one?" The question had been haunting him.

John did a double-take. "The one? Oh, yes, he's the one alright. God revealed to me the sign to watch for. And then one day…" He scratched his beard and looked thoughtfully at Andrew. "In fact, it was shortly before you first joined up. One day my cousin Jesus showed up, down from Nazareth. Hadn't seen him in years. We hugged and talked about how long it'd been. Then he said, 'I'm here to be baptized.' Well, even then I knew he was a better man than me, and I said he should baptize me. But he insisted. So I dunked him."

The circle of men nodded. They'd heard the story before, but they never tired of it.

"That's when I knew. Before my eyes, God's sign of the Messiah… The Holy Spirit came down—looked just like a dove—and settled on Jesus. The Son of God, dripping with muddy Jordon water. I knew then…I'd just baptized the Messiah!"

Everyone started talking and asking questions all at once. Andrew withdrew into his thoughts.

Yes, he'd heard the story before. But doubts danced with expectation in his heart. The fulfillment of God's plan, awaited by millions of God's people for thousands of years. Was he finally here? Was this carpenter's son from a disreputable backwater town truly the fulfillment of the ages? The goal toward which all of Israel's hundreds of patriarchs and judges and kings and prophets had been pointing? The answer to all the centuries of grief and hope—miracles and disasters, blessings and warnings, wars and empires and exiles and restorations?

Did they all finally lead to Jesus?

– – –

Next morning, John, Andrew, and Thomas, another of John's disciples, rose at dawn, ate sparingly, and made their way to the riverside. The crowd was larger than ever. John preached from a three-foot-high mound until noon. Then he came down to the river and began baptizing the repentant. Hundreds were lined up. When John became tired, Andrew and Thomas helped.

At about four in the afternoon, John climbed back up on the mound to preach until dusk. He was starting to straighten when he froze, his gaze fixed over the heads of the crowd. "The Lamb of God," he whispered. He stood on his toes, pointing and shouting, "There he is! The Lamb of God who takes away the sin of the world!"

Andrew quickly climbed up on the mound and squinted in the direction John pointed.

A hand grasped his ankle. "Do you see him?" asked Thomas from below.

"Yes," said Andrew breathlessly. "Let's go."

Together they shoved between the bodies, frantic to reach Jesus before he was gone. The crowd thinned, and they gazed up the road that led away from the river. Among the handful of people on the road, one stood out,

> "Come and see for yourselves."

even when viewed from behind. The figure walked with the confidence of a king, but not the arrogance of a temple priest. He was tall, with muscular arms and back, accustomed to hard work.

Andrew and Thomas ran. As they neared, Jesus heard their footfalls and turned. They both stopped, breathing heavily, dripping sweat.

Jesus' face was also moist from the heat. His brown eyes—underscored by dark semicircles, as though he hadn't slept well—were calm, commanding, inviting, questioning.

"What are you after?" he asked.[40]

Andrew glanced at Thomas, whose gaze remained fixed on Jesus.

"Teacher—" Thomas began, then faltered.

Andrew swallowed. "Teacher…wh—where are you staying?"

Jesus smiled, sized them up, then answered, "Come and see for yourselves." He turned and continued walking with that unhurried gait.

The next several hours were imprinted on Andrew's memory for life—his first taste of Jesus' Presence. John was impressive, but this man was one of a kind. Hanging out with him was refreshing, challenging, enlivening, clarifying… Indefinably normal. Frightening in a fascinating way.

It was the first day of a thousand. Their friendship deepened.

Three years later, the Messiah was dead.

Another three days, and he lived again.

Finally, Jesus went back to heaven and sent his Holy Spirit, as he'd promised. And although Andrew felt sorrow for Jesus' physical absence, he soon realized he'd started hanging out with his friend again. It was almost like that first day all over again. In some ways it was better. Andrew missed his face, his voice, his strong hand grasping an arm. But the most important parts of the friendship remained unchanged: the patient listening ear; the forgiving, accepting heart; the warm encouragement; the firm challenges; the great questions; the guidance; the hope; the truth.

And just as before, every time they were together, in some way Andrew came away changed.

Brief Debrief

Dwell in Jesus' Presence as you dig into these questions and write in your *Pray21 Journal*. Include him in your thoughts, ask him questions, listen. Share your thoughts and plans with your partners, and continue prayerfully supporting each other.

- Have you ever wished you could have been with Jesus in the flesh? How would that have been better?

- What's better about the kind of relationship you can have with him now? Today, how deep can a person's friendship with Christ go?

- What do you do to spend time with Jesus? Does it help you understand him better, or allow you to be more open to him?

- What's something new or something more that you want to do to deepen your friendship with him? What's your first step?

SECURE CHANNEL

Jesus, how well do I really know you? I think if I knew you better, I'd be more and more hungry to connect with you. Because you're the best friend anyone ever had.

I'm sorry for the things and people I've made more important than you in my life. Help me make time for you. I need it. I need you! Change me. And then as I go about my other activities and relationships, make me aware of your Presence all the time.

I pray, too, for your deepening connection with [name your partners]. Pull them closer, and make them more like you.

BACKGROUND FILES

To learn more about enjoying Jesus' Presence, read John 1:15–51; 15:1–17; Acts 4:13; 1 John 1:1.

PART 3:

BECOME

Have you ever anticipated a growth change in yourself, only to find it wasn't happening nearly as fast as you thought it would? You've probably also had times when you've become so discouraged with your pace of growth that you gave up and thought, *I'm not changing at all.*

The truth is that anyone who's pursuing Jesus and honestly seeking to live for him is changing. No heart that stays focused on him can remain the same. But no one changes completely in a day. Or a week. Or a decade. The life of the most committed, most obedient Jesus-follower is a life of continual learning and growth.

It takes diligence and work, contrary to the common misconception that we simply sit back and let God do it all. And it takes complete dependence on God, contrary to the equally common fallacy that we do it all ourselves. The Godward life is filled with mistakes. And humility. And forgiveness. And risks. And hard times. And strength that increases through hardship.

And the further into this life you go, the more you realize you wouldn't trade it for anything.

Whether you expect your spiritual journey toward eternity to last seven more days or seventy more years, let's look at a few growth dynamics to anticipate as you live a life that counts for Christ.

are you really listening?

Adam and Eve, just outside Eden: *God said, "Not that tree. Anything else is fine." But no. We bought the snake's story. God made it so easy. Why didn't we listen?*[41]

Noah's neighbor, chin-deep in rainwater: *Noah warned us. God's judgment was coming. He invited us on his boat. I wish we'd listened.*[42]

Mr. Iscariot, just informed of his son Judas's suicide: *I should have known greed would be the end of my boy. I heard the Scriptures every Sabbath, "Point your kids in the right direction," but I was too busy with my career to listen.*[43]

A grieving nineteen-year-old, AD 2007: *I knew it was all wrong. The Bible says so, but I also knew so. I partied, I drank, I took drugs, I drove, and now my two best friends are dead. Why didn't I listen?*

God is talking to everyone on earth. Especially those who know the Bible. But even those who don't:

- "By taking a long and thoughtful look at what God has created, people have always been able to see what their eyes as such can't see: eternal power, for instance, and the mystery of his divine being. So nobody has a good excuse."[44]

- "When outsiders who have never heard of God's law follow it more or less by instinct, they confirm its truth by their obedience. They show that God's law is not something alien, imposed on us from without, but woven into the very fabric of our creation. There is something deep within them that echoes God's yes and no, right and wrong."[45]

We've all come into the world equipped with spiritual "ears," capable of recognizing God and his truth. That's why Jesus so often issued challenges like "Anyone with ears to hear should listen and understand."[46] Or as the Bible paraphrase *The Message* interprets it, "Are you listening to this? Really listening?"

More than a thousand years before Jesus spoke those words, God's ear was compassionately open to a woman named Hannah. She couldn't get pregnant, so she begged God for a child. If he'd give her a son, she promised to give him back for lifelong service at the Tabernacle, Israel's worship center.

And along came a boy named Samuel, whose name sounds like the Hebrew phrase "heard by God." It's fitting that Sam became a listener.

When Sam was about three, his parents brought him to live permanently at the Tabernacle with the high priest Eli. And Sam grew up like you and me, but with a heart and an ear devoted to God.

He became like Eli's third son. Which was good, because Eli's first two sons, Hophni and Phinehas, didn't turn out so well. They "helped" with the worship services, stealing sacrifices that people had brought for God, sleeping with female Tabernacle assistants, and otherwise making a mockery of God. Eli tried talking them out of it, but he failed to take responsibility as their father or their boss. He should have fired them. But, then, he enjoyed his share of the proceeds as well.

Guess how God felt.

God sent multiple warnings to Eli. First through the Scriptures, which clearly described the character and duties of his priests, as well as stories of his

"I'm your servant, ready to listen."

severe dealings with those who treated him with disrespect. God also sent a message to Eli through a prophet: "You're honoring your sons above me, treating my sacrifices like your personal property. Your whole family is suffering because of this, and both of your sons will die on the same day."

Still Eli did nothing.

Young Sam had been serving the Lord several years when one night he was dropping off to sleep. "Samuel." He sat up and looked around. No one in sight. Must have been Eli calling for something. So he ran to Eli's room. "I'm right here. You called?"

Eli himself was startled awake, and said foggily, "No, not me. Go back to bed, my boy."

Sam obeyed, only to have it happen again. "Samuel." He ran to Eli, and was sent back to bed.

He was settling in once again, when… "Samuel." A third time he checked in with Eli, but this time the old man knew something weird was going on. So he told Sam, "Go back to bed, but if someone calls again, answer, 'Speak, God. I'm your servant, ready to listen.'"[47]

This was all strange and new to Sam. But he lay back down.

"Samuel, Samuel." His eyes grew wide. He knew from legend that the double repetition meant God had a very important message.

"Speak," he said. "I'm your servant, ready to listen."[48]

And God gave Sam one last message to pass along to the old priest. Eli and his sons had pushed God too far, and all the consequences he'd warned about would soon come true.

Sam was in no hurry to get up next morning. He had some heavy mail to deliver. But Eli summoned him and ordered him to quote God's message word for word. When Sam did, Eli just sighed and said, "It's what the Lord has decided to do, and he knows best." Eli must have closed his heart long ago.

So, while Eli's family waited for God's judgment, Sam kept on growing taller and stronger and closer to God. Throughout Israel, he gained a reputation of respect as God's prophet, because everything he said was right on target. Flawless.

The day came when Hophni and Phinehas died in a battle with the idolatrous Philistines who lived nearby. When news arrived, Eli fell back in shock, broke his neck, and died.

Sam stepped in as Israel's leader, ears wide open to God. First thing, he purified the nation, which had wandered a long way from God's instructions. He made them get rid of their idols and led them in national repentance. Once they got right with the Lord, they were able to defend themselves against the hostile nations around them, and Israel had peace and security.

Up to this point, Israel had no king—just spiritual and military leaders. But in the right timing God spoke. Sam listened and became Israel's "king maker." Under God's guidance, he put King Saul into office. When

Saul proved a poor listener and angered God with his disobedience, Sam was led to a young shepherd named David—youngest of several brothers. Only someone with ears to hear God would have made the right choice. Because of Sam's finely tuned reception, God raised up Israel's greatest king ever. Until, that is, the day when King Jesus assumes the throne.[49]

Such a big difference between "Why didn't I listen?" and "At your service, Lord."

God is always speaking. Time for a hearing check?

Brief Debrief

Speak and listen to God as you work through and journal about these questions. Sometimes God speaks through your partners, so keep your ears open when you connect with them. If you have something encouraging or challenging for them, share it in love. Maybe they need to listen, too.

- How well have you been listening to God lately? What makes listening hard for you?

- Describe one time you listened well, or a time you wish you had listened better. What happened?

- How can you tell the difference between truth from God— through any avenue of communication—and something that's not his truth?

- What is one thing you think God is trying to tell you now?

- How, specifically, will you show him in word and action that you're really listening?

Secure Channel

Speak, Lord, because I honestly want to hear you. But my "ear"—my heart—gets plugged up with fear, laziness, pride, greed, and more. [Tell him what makes listening hard for you.]

Please change me so I'm more open to you, willing to accept what's hard to accept, and do what's hard to do. I want to talk with you so much and pay such close attention to your truth that you'll always come through loud and clear. Help me trust you so well that I'll obey you without hesitation. This week, to show my love I'll... [tell him your commitment].

I pray the same for [name your partners]. Help them experience the joy of hearing and obeying you without resistance.

BACKGROUND FILES

To learn more about listening carefully to God, read 1 Samuel 1–4, 7; Psalm 19; Isaiah 6:8–10; Mark 4:23–25; James 1:19–25.

who do you say I am?

The world is full of christs. If you interviewed one hundred people, you'd get fifty different versions of Jesus. Even the Messiah's true followers believe in an amazing variety of editions of their Lord.

Will the real Jesus please stand up? (Or create a new planet if you prefer.)

Satan, our enemy, is a master at taking something true and counterfeiting it. Just the right blend of truth and lie to keep Person A from finding salvation. Mix the right words with the wrong meanings, and Believer B will end up ineffective for life. Fill "Jesus" with enough reality to make him credible, and you can fill the rest with anything you want.

The different christs appeal to different people's particular presuppositions, preferences, and profit incentives. Some misconception, a certain past injury, or a strong vested interest might predispose you to lean toward a shade of falsehood you *want* to be true. Along comes the color-coordinated jesus to give you an extra shove away from the truth, claiming God's authority to boot.

Even those who have a handle on the authentic Jesus must work hard not to lose him. Especially those who come into fame, money, power, or any of life's other addictions and distractions. There's a jesus that promotes each of those, and if we're not diligent, we can let an intruder push aside the Messiah we once worshiped.

Jesus asked his disciples, "Who do you say I am?" And Peter got it right: "You're the Christ, the Messiah, the Son of the living God."[50]

When the temple guards came to arrest Jesus, he asked, "Who is it you want?" They seemed to understand: "Jesus of Nazareth."[51] But his answer—translated literally, "I AM," the Old Testament name of God Almighty—blew the guards over backward to the ground. Apparently they weren't ready for the genuine article.[52]

Soft Focus

At some time or other, Jesus confronts all of us: "Who do you say I am?" Al Hollingsworth has had to answer that question many times. Sometimes he's gotten it right. Sometimes not. His track record is a lot better these days than it used to be.

He grew up in Baptist church circles, but wasn't really interested in Jesus. He played guard and tackle on the University of Colorado football team, anticipating an NFL career. One day Jesus got Al's attention while he slept—he was knocked unconscious, that is—for about ten minutes during a football game. Since Al wasn't doing anything else at the moment, God spoke to him, telling Al he would serve God's mission as a successful businessman—a rare thing for an African American in the early 1960s.

Al had faced the real Jesus, and he woke up *motivated*. He went from borderline flunking to honor roll. After college, he brushed off the NFL and pursued God's calling, breaking into the hard-to-enter paper industry and, as God promised, starting a successful business.

However, by this time, Al had unknowingly switched messiahs. In his words, "I began saying, 'Just a minute, God. Let me take care of this deal. Then I'll be with you. I'll be right there.'" Instead of the Jesus who was completely sufficient, Al now listened to the Supplement-My-Sufficiency christ, who encouraged do-it-yourself me-dependence.

A beautiful young employee named Hattie soon became Al's life partner in marriage. Meanwhile, Al pushed and manipulated his own way toward success.

> Work hard at staying locked in on the Son of the living God.

And suffered a heart attack. Broken by this crisis, Al recognized the false messiah he'd created and invited the true Jesus back as CEO. He recovered, but later discovered he'd once again left Jesus in the dust. He and Hattie recommitted and prayed, "Lord, whatever you don't want in our lives, please take it away."

So God bankrupted their business. And saved Al from an unseen danger. It turned out that the Identity-in-Doing jesus had been lurking on the premises, coaxing Al to define himself by his career, rather than by his Lord.

Crystal Clear

Devastated, Al nonetheless did the right thing. He pursued Jesus with everything in him, retreating to the countryside for months, trying to hear God. He'd stopped trusting his own heart—a wise move if your heart is aimed the wrong direction. But once Al set his sights on the genuine Jesus, God taught him that he could trust his desires, because they were now God's desires.

Al's desire? To make a business comeback. This time under God, by God, and for God. That's what they did—God and Al, in that order—twenty-seven years ago. Founded on a solid history and an enduring reputation, the multimillion-dollar Aldelano Packaging Corporation now employs several hundred—sometimes over a thousand—people in five states and serves numerous Fortune 500 clients, like Verizon, General Mills, Proctor & Gamble, and Toyota. When you buy a packaged product, these companies make the inside, and Al's company wraps it in the outside, as well as providing other services. Al and his business receive frequent honors from, among others, the US Department of Commerce and the National Minority Supplier Development Council.

The counterfeit christs haven't stopped pestering Al. They're continually vying for his worship. Al and Hattie, together, work hard at staying locked in on the Son of the living God.

They've started using their business for the purpose of doing God's business. They've developed biblically based training programs to show how Christ's truth spills over into success in every area of life—personal confidence, business, impact on people, anything. One program for young people is called BOSS (Building On Spiritual Substance) the Movement. Another, for adults, is the Vertical Leap Seminar.

Through these programs, Al and Hattie help people of all ages fight off counterfeit christs. For example, by teaching Spirit-guided self-confidence and godly self-esteem, they expose the Salvation-by-Scumhood jesus. This false messiah is eternally disgusted with every human and can only redeem us if we admit we're worthless and always will be. He denies the beautiful image of God in the individual, as well as the shining new creation who emerges at salvation—both crafted lovingly by the Maker.

By equipping young people with business skills and teaching that financial success can be a tool for God's kingdom, Al and Hattie are combating the Shun-the-World christ and replacing him with the true Jesus, who wants us to use his earthly blessings for his work. By advocating Spirit-dependent hard work, they're confronting the Sit-Back-and-Let-Me-Do-Everything messiah, who says the word "faith" means "passivity."

The Hollingsworths steer inner-city kids away from "success" in drug culture and gangs, where the Dominate-the-Weak jesus reigns, and introduce them to the Jesus who defines success as caring for the weak. They replace the Don't-Think-Ahead christ with the Christ who says, "Dream big with me." They push out the cowardly Play-It-Safe lord, and welcome the Lord who stands by us while we take risks of obedient faith.[53]

The world is filled with christs. They don't care which you choose, as long as it's not the Jesus of the Bible. Who's been knocking at your door? Whispering in your ear? Running your life?

Jesus is asking, "Who do you say I am?"

Your answer?

BRIEF DEBRIEF

Meet with Jesus and talk over these questions with him, recording your thoughts in your *Pray21 Journal.* Help your partners think clearly about Jesus and live for him. Let them help you, too.

- Describe the false jesus who most easily fools you when you let your guard down.

- How is the real Christ different and better?

- Who do you say Jesus is? Choose an answer that zeroes in on the Truth[54] and clearly sets him off from the fakes. Your answer can be as long or short as you need.

- Name one visible difference your Lord will make in your life this week.

SECURE CHANNEL

Jesus, the One and Only, Lord of all lords, I'm deciding now to worship you, only you. I've followed counterfeits before. They don't love me, they've never helped me. Thank you for always being there for me. Thanks for letting me see you.

Teach me discipline to keep my eyes and heart on you. Expose clearly the lies that try to distract me. Protect me. Make me so familiar with your voice that I can't mistake any other voice for yours. And help me show my devotion this week by [tell him one new commitment].

Please also show yourself clearly to [name your partners]. Help them reject the fakes who claim your name.

BACKGROUND FILES

To learn more about telling Jesus apart from the imposters, read Matthew 16:13–20; John 10:1–33; 18:1–8; 1 John 4:1–8.

who doesn't first figure the cost?

Josh Weidmann—pastor, speaker, author, and radio broadcaster—has spent his life defining a very important word. But in order to understand what he's discovered, let's take a brief detour through Hollywood.

Maybe you've seen the 1986 movie, *Crocodile Dundee*. The title character, Michael J. "Crocodile" Dundee, is an expert at surviving in the Australian outback. He visits New York City and discovers it's as wild a jungle as any in the world.

In one scene he's threatened by a mugger with a switchblade. His lady friend warns, "Mick…he's got a knife."

Dundee narrows his sun-wizened eyes, laughs, and says in his easygoing Australian accent, "Tha's no' a knoif." He produces a wicked-looking twelve-inch hunting blade—a veritable sword—and holds it up, turning it back and forth. "*That's* a knoif."

The mugger runs.

Jesus used this approach once in his teaching. Large crowds were traveling around with him. Too large.

So he decided to stop and teach. "You want to be disciples? Okay. Time for a test. You love your families. Good. But do you love me so much that your love for your family—for your very life—looks like hatred by comparison? If not, *you're not a disciple*. Not one of mine."

Many listeners frowned and glanced around.

"I'll require you to carry a cross and follow me with it to the place where you'll be nailed to it, beside me. Will you do that? No? Then you're not disciple material."

Several started weaving their way to the edge of the audience and walked away.

Jesus wasn't finished. "If you were building a house, wouldn't you first get out your spreadsheet and figure the cost to see if you can afford it? Otherwise, you might lay the foundation, run out of money, and it's game over. Everyone will mock you: 'That's not a house. And you're not a builder.'

"Or a king goes to war. Wouldn't he first calculate whether he can beat the other army, twice the size of his? If he can't, he'll wave the white flag, pleading, 'I'm no warrior. Can't we just get along?'"

Jesus scanned the thinning crowd. Many of those who remained were looking worried. Time to finish weeding.

"I expect you to give up everything for me. Anyone who won't—holding back the least breadcrumb—that's not a disciple."

Only a fraction of the crowd remained—some shaking and sweating, nervously watching all the retreating backs. But they stayed.

Jesus broke into a broad grin. He walked to the nearest man and hugged him. He kissed the cheek of a sobbing woman who refused to leave, bent down and tweaked the stomach of a young boy. Then he stood in their midst, spread his arms, and turned, taking them all into his rotating view. "Now, *these... These* are disciples."

Jesus demands everything.

Unreasonable? Unrealistic? Josh Weidmann doesn't think so. Josh's journey with Christ started at age four, when he decided to make Jesus his Savior *and* Lord. Once he understood the options, nothing else made sense. For Josh, nothing else ever has.

Three years later he started following in his late grandfather's footsteps, sharing Christ with groups through gospel magic. And so a seven-year-old chose a disciple's path. Through his early years, his teens, and now young adulthood, over and over Josh has been confronted with the price tag that Jesus puts on discipleship—everything you have—and has shaken hands on the deal every time, thinking, *What a bargain!*

> "I obey God because I can't do anything else."

But he didn't foresee the particulars of what discipleship meant for him. "At almost every turn," he says, "the path I've traveled was unexpected. I wanted to be a great singer—the next Michael W. Smith. But God took me a different direction."

He didn't expect to help launch a prayer group in his Colorado school, but that's what God (and Josh, in that order) did. That expanded into a plan to start prayer and Bible groups in every school in his state, then every school in the nation—a movement called the Revival Generation.

He never dreamed he'd testify before the Colorado legislature in favor of school prayer and the Ten Commandments in the classroom.

And when he woke on April 20, 1999, he certainly didn't plan to spend his school day under lock-down, worrying about the lives of his friends at Columbine High School four miles away. In the aftermath, Josh naturally fell into a community leadership role coordinating the spiritual healing of thousands, speaking through the media to a traumatized nation, sharing Christ with countless seekers.

Josh would have laughed if you'd said he'd write a book. "I never got better than a D in English," he admits. "But now I'm working on my second and third books."

National speaking tours? Daily radio broadcasts? Moody Bible Institute? Pastor? Ministry website (www.joshweidmann.com)? Josh didn't expect any of these until God (and Josh) did them. But because Josh is sold out, he takes on whatever tasks God puts in front of him. And he does it with a smile.

"I obey God because I can't do anything else. I've never seen any other reason for living that made sense. I tell young people, 'You've got to do this. What does your life amount to if you're not adding to the kingdom of the Lord? Make your life count for something bigger than yourself.'"

Josh is human; he routinely deals with doubts. "My first reaction to the idea of ministry was, *That's a cool thing, but not for me. I don't have the talent.* Sometimes I still think that." His writing was another area of insecurity. "But God keeps opening doors, then giving me the strength and ability. The old saying goes, 'God doesn't call the equipped—he equips the called.' God calls me to do something, and then he equips me along the way in ways I never thought possible."

Josh acknowledges another weakness. After the Columbine shooting, he saw the spiritual need and he (and God, in that order) frantically set about trying to meet it. He assumed, *If I don't do it, it won't get done.*

"I let my schoolwork go. My junior and senior years I got a 2.01 grade point average—I barely graduated. I thought it was total abandonment to God. But my mentor sat me down and said, 'Josh, you think God needs you. He doesn't. God could do all of this without you. He could write a message in the sky and save all these souls. God *allows* you the privilege of being his servant.'"

Josh's motives were largely good, but he realized he'd shifted into a partly self-focused mindset. He'd made himself big and God small. So he went back to the truth—big God, small people. Truth he continually strives to remember today.

Josh is an ordinary young man. But an extraordinary God challenged him: "Hand it all over. Deal or no deal?" Josh said, "Deal!" That's why God is working miracles through his life. Just as he can through yours.

And *that*, by the way, is a disciple.

BRIEF DEBRIEF

If you take these questions seriously, the outcome could be expensive. And the returns will be beyond your dreams. Journal thoughtfully and prayerfully, and interact with an open heart with your partners, young and old.

- What, if anything, keeps you from selling out to God? Something "better"? Fear of pain or loss? Be specific.

- Brainstorm several benefits of living for God. Consider how much each of them really means.

- Selling out is risky. How does God promise to reimburse, protect, and strengthen you?

- Write your gift list to God. What does "everything" include in your life?

- How you will go about giving him his first gift from your list?

SECURE CHANNEL

(Gulp.) Everything, Lord? Carry a cross to my own execution? This is really tough. The only reason I'm considering it is because of you. Selling out doesn't make total sense to me. But your steady love, your flawless wisdom, your absolute power—these are starting to make sense. And the huge cost is starting to look smaller in comparison to you.

I want to be your disciple. Give me desire to accept the cost. I want to learn to pay it gladly. Show me your hand at work. Give me reassurance and confidence.

And do the same for [name your partners]. Show us how to help each other stay sold out to you.

BACKGROUND FILES

To learn more about the cost and benefit of being Jesus' disciple, read Luke 6:43–49; 14:25–33; Matthew 10.

do you want to get well?

I was only eleven when the donkey kicked me in the back. When my legs stopped working.

When I got too big for my parents to manhandle, they brought me to the covered Bethesda pool, up in north Jerusalem, and left me there for "the community" to look after. The "residents" who were already there—the blind, the paralyzed, the whole list—helped me learn how to beg for each day's food. How to take care of personal necessities. How to stay warm. For decades I lived that life.

Why did Dad and Mom bring me to the pool? To be healed, of course. Or haven't you heard the legend? Okay, it goes like this. Every so often an angel stirs the water. When it happens, the first person into the pool gets healed.

I think I've seen a few stirrings. At first I tried to drag myself to the water, but I never made it first. I begged anyone who'd listen to stay and help me, just in case the angel showed up. But no one would stick around for a legend. Or for someone as worthless as me.

Sometimes, when most of us were sleeping, someone would scream out, "Look! The angel is here!" just as a joke.

I never saw any angel.

And I never saw anyone actually get healed.

Sometimes doctors would show up and put in a little pro bono time. It made them look good to the Pharisees. Maybe they got their tithe reduced to five percent that way. I don't know. I never paid them much attention. When they came, I pretended to sleep, and they would move on to the next guy.

One day I was doing what I did best—feeling sorry for myself—when a guy walked in. He dressed like a teacher. And a bunch of people came crowding in after him. I was amazed that one of his followers was my old begging buddy Shemuel.

Shemuel saw me. Last time he was here, he was blind.

He'd never seen my face before, but he figured out who I was. He grabbed the teacher's arm and said something. The teacher looked right at me. Suddenly I was scared. Something about his face. Not mad. But intense, focused, powerful. And I could tell he really liked me.

He said it like it was going to happen.

That scared me. For the first time in thirty-eight years, I didn't know what was going to happen next.

He crouched down beside me. I was shaking, so he put his hand on my arm. And he said, "Do you want to get well?"

All of a sudden I wasn't afraid—I was mad.

I laughed in his face and rolled my eyes. What kind of idiot walks up to a cripple and asks if he wanted to get well? "Of course I want to get well," I retorted.

He paused, then asked, "Do you really?"

The dread returned. I felt cornered. "Well...what would you do if you had no one to help you into the pool when the water stirs? I try my best, all by myself, but someone else always beats me to it." I didn't mention that it never did anyone any good. "So don't waste your time on me. Go help someone else." I sounded like a whiner, even to me.

"Get up."

He said it like it was *going* to happen. Like no one had any business thinking it wouldn't. As though the words themselves would do the trick.

And I changed inside. For the first time in thirty-eight years, I *really did* want to get well.

"Get up," he said again. "Pick up your bedroll and walk."

So I did.

Now, some people would have run out of there whooping and leaping. Not me. I was more scared than ever. What's more, I walked right out into a swarm of Pharisees.

Why was I carrying my bedroll on the Sabbath? they asked.

Because a guy healed me and said to.

Who was he?

I was stuck. I never got the teacher's name. And now he and his people cluster were gone.

I went to the temple. (Maybe God would help me find direction.) And who should be there, but the teacher!

Before I could get away, he caught up and said, "I see you're making good use of your new equipment." My legs did feel great. "In case you're wondering, I'm Jesus. And it's time for you to stop sinning."

"Sinning?" I couldn't believe my ears. "How could I sin? All my life I've been lying around helpless."

Jesus nodded. "Exactly."

And then I knew. My "helplessness" was sin. I thought I was humbling myself and depending on God, like the Scriptures say. But all those years, God wanted me to depend on him...*and do something.* I did nothing. I robbed him.

I couldn't look Jesus in the eye.

"I'm sorry, Lord. I didn't know." I started to gush. "But I'm still afraid. What do I do now? I never planned on this."

He touched my arm, like he did before. It helped. "I know you're scared. But you're a capable adult. You have been for a long time. Start taking responsibility. Your widowed mother could use some help. How about starting there?"

I stared at him, astonished. How did he know?

He chuckled. "Make something of this life God has given you. You're worth a lot to him. And so are your remaining years." His smile changed to concern. "Don't misuse what's left, or something worse than a physical handicap might happen to you."

I promised. He left.

Then I tried to remember the way to my mother's home.

On the way, I ran into those same Pharisees. I told them who healed me. They got mad and took away my bedroll.

I used to think only my legs needed strength. But that's nothing compared to the strength my spirit has needed from God since that first, new day. Strength to resist self-pity. Strength to take care of my mother, even though she still treats me like a crippled child. Strength to start making a real living in the real world.

I love using my legs. But most of my paying jobs are ones I could have done, with or without legs, for the last thirty-eight years. Weaving. Mending clothes and blankets. Things like that.

And every chance I get, I tell people about Jesus. I don't get paid for that. I don't need to.

I can't help wondering. What if I'd asked God for healing when I was eleven? Or twenty? Or thirty-one? Maybe he would have said yes a long time ago.

And even if he'd still left me lame for thirty-eight years, what good things could I have done with two strong arms, a good head, a tongue that could speak truth and encouragement? How much of my mission did I sacrifice while I kept my spirit crippled? Paralyzed.

Because I was afraid to get well.

BRIEF DEBRIEF

As you wrestle with these questions, be especially honest. With God…with your partners…with yourself. Use your *Pray21 Journal* as a sounding board. Use your partners as a source of prayer and encouragement. And be the same for them.

- A huge number of people, young and old, have emotional and spiritual illnesses and wounds inside. Pain from abuse, rejection, or neglect. Horrible self-image. Destructive habits and addictions. Depression… A lot of people prefer to stay sick. Why? What good do they think they're getting out of their condition?

- Do you know someone who doesn't want to get well? Don't mention names. How might Jesus try talking them into accepting his healing?

- How about you? Are you resisting God's healing in some way? Do you know why?

- How might your life be different if you let him make you well?

- What specific steps would lead to your healing? (Consider, for example, prayer, confession, accountability, learning God's truth, getting counseling or rehab.) What do you want to do first?

 ### Secure Channel

Lord, you've taken care of me in so many ways. [Thank him for specifics.]

But I've held back some of my favorite wounds and sicknesses from your healing touch. I don't completely understand my weird attachment to them. But here they are. [Open them up to him.]

I do want to be well. Completely well. Give me patience with the time it takes. Give me courage for the obedience it takes. Give me humility to be vulnerable and honest. And give me confidence that you still love me, no matter what I dig up inside.

Fix me, so I can know you and serve you better.

[Remember to pray for your partners' complete healing, too.]

Background Files

To learn more about the courage to accept God's healing, read John 3:19–21; 5:1–18; 1 Corinthians 1:25–31; 1 Thessalonians 5:14.

two-week
checkpoint

The marathon is two-thirds over. Seven more days to go. Let's take a breather and talk about your progress and plans so far.

In Part 1 of your Pray21 venture, you were challenged to *Believe*. To believe in yourself the way God believes in you. To believe in the *you* he made—equipped with the gifts and abilities he has given you, empowered and guided by his presence with you, a child of God, deepening a forever friendship with Jesus. It's true, in yourself you don't have all you need. But when you bring all you have to God, he works miracles through you. *Believe*.

In Part 2, you were reminded that you *Belong*. God wanted you, he chose you, he treasures you, and you're part of his mission. Your real home is heaven, and you'll get there. But during your short stay here on this beautiful, sin-filled planet, no matter what you've done, no matter who you've become, he still wants you. Get right with him as often as it takes, and stay connected with other believers. Get on with the mission. Hang out with Jesus every day. *Belong*.

Now you're well into Part 3, and you're learning what it means to *Become*. To become a mature, complete Christ-follower is to humbly open your ears and heart to God, even for the things you don't want to hear. It's choosing the Christ of the Bible, not the Christ of popular opinion or personal preference. It's giving everything to God, and obeying him in truth, not just in word. It's accepting his healing, taking risks in obedience, and sometimes trusting him even while you're taking some serious hits. All this to *Become*.

Meet with God and with your partners to work through these checkpoint questions. Be willing to give and receive help and ideas, whether you're younger or older, as you process your commitments together. And record your responses in your *Pray21 Journal.*

1. How are you feeling at this stage? Tired? Pumped? Scared? Important? Something else? Do you know why?

2. In one or two sentences, how are you now seeing the bigger picture of God's mission for his people on earth?

3. In one or two sentences, summarize your current understanding of God's call for you as a specialist on assignment in that mission.

4. How have your partners been helpful to you this week? How have you helped them?

5. Review all you've read, considered, and discussed during this second week (Days 8–14). What is the one new step of growth and obedience you think God wants you to take? It might be brand new for you, or it might be raising the bar on an existing goal. (It might even be one of your "leftover" dream goals from Question 7 in the One-Week Checkpoint.)

6. **Rubber Meets the Road:** Write down the necessary particulars that you need for true follow-through on your commitment. Be sure to include a plan for support and accountability from others. And be sure you have a way of determining whether you're accomplishing your goal. Take a real risk, but keep your commitment real (within your reach to achieve).

7. From Days 8–14, what other growth areas, goals, or commitments would you like to pursue some day? Write them down as reminders for later.

should I beg for escape?

Walk through the door of Tammy Trent's home, and immediately your attention will be pulled—as if by a magnet—to a larger-than-life painting on the wall. The breathtaking blue ocean and the sun splashing across the view draw you in.

Then you'll see her. A young woman with blonde hair stands on the veranda, gazing out to sea. Beside her is a table, one chair, one letter, and one rose. She's looking for something.

This beautiful painting was a gift to Tammy, painted by a close friend in the summer of 2000. It was entitled "To Remember." How could she have known that, just a year later, this painting would come to life?

Down

Tammy and Trent (from whom she takes her stage name) began their relationship in high school. During the first few years it had its on-again-off-again moments. But when they married in 1990, it was definitely on. For good.

Tammy launched into her career as a singer and songwriter. Trent served as her manager. For eleven years, aside from her Lord, her husband was everything to Tammy.

One of Trent's hobbies was free diving—underwater exploration without an air tank. He trained thoroughly and took careful precautions. One September day, on a part-vacation, part-missions trip, Trent pushed off into Jamaica's spectacular Blue Lagoon, promising to be back in fifteen minutes. Tammy settled back to enjoy the sun.

Forty-five minutes later, Tammy knew something was wrong. Trent hadn't come back. Some of the locals helped her search. The authorities became involved. At nightfall there was no sign of Trent.

That horrifying day was September 10, 2001—the day Tammy's world changed. The rest of the world would change tomorrow.

Tammy emerged the next morning to TV coverage of global chaos, images of airliners crashing into towers and military headquarters. Trent's body was discovered moments later.

Only Trent's father was able to board a plane before the terrorist attack and the grounding of all US flights. He came to her side in Jamaica and took over all the practical arrangements. But she longed for her mother's embrace. A voice over the phone wasn't nearly enough.

Throughout her life, Mom had always been there. Her encouragement gave Tammy confidence as a child to get up on stage and perform. Tammy went on to pour herself into basketball, becoming a drummer, and eventually cutting commercial CDs. Her mom was her most faithful prayer partner.

But now Tammy needed touch. She felt abandoned in a strange place—the place where her husband had been torn from her.

Back

What do you do when your world shatters? When the full weight of the blow crushes down on you? When your pain and loss is so unbearable that

"I want your will to be done, not mine."

you're literally going to go out of your mind? There's no fix, no escape, no rest.

That's exactly where Jesus was one April night. He was facing the imminent loss of a Loved One. His Father. It would happen the next day—the day the world would change.

Jesus had known for some time that his mission was to die. And he wanted to do it; that's how great Love was. But it didn't make the doing any easier. He could see his future—the near-fatal flogging, the torturously fatal crucifixion. But even worse was the prospect of losing his Father.

Tammy lost Trent after eleven years of marriage. That's a heart-rending tragedy. The Son was about to lose the Father after an eternity of absolute, flawless intimacy. A worldful of sin would be smeared over the spotless soul of the Messiah. The Almighty would curse his Son and turn his back. The Trinity would be ripped down the middle.

That's unimaginable.

No wonder Jesus was so deeply stressed that he literally bled through his sweat pores.[55] We can see why he said things like, "My soul is crushed with grief to the point of death."[56]

Who would have blamed Jesus if he begged for a way out, in the face of insanity-making pain and loss? No one would. In fact, Jesus did pray repeatedly, pleading with the Father to find some other way to accomplish the mission.[57] But in the end, the panic, the frantic terror—none of it kept Jesus from saying, "I want your will to be done, not mine"[58]

Jesus' disciple John, one of his best friends, was there when Jesus spilled his fear on the table: "Right now I am storm-tossed. And what am I going to say? 'Father, get me out of this'?" He had every right. But instead he continued, "No, this is why I came in the first place. I'll say, 'Father, put your glory on display.'"[59]

As desperately as Jesus hated what was coming—even though he allowed himself the luxury of an hour to sink down into fear—he ultimately stood up and got back on with the mission. He knew exactly what it was: "At this moment the world is in crisis. Now Satan, the ruler of this world, will be thrown out. And I, as I am lifted up from the earth [on the cross], will attract everyone to me and gather them around me."[60]

Up

Trent's death did a serious number on Tammy. It would on anyone. For days she could do nothing but hurt. God understood. Everyone understood.

But before long, while she was still stranded in Jamaica, she found her voice—the shaky but unmistakable voice of faith. She told God how much she hurt. And even though she didn't have any clue about the whys, she knew the Who. She said, "I trust you."

"When you're absolutely broken," says Tammy, "and you don't know the right prayer, the right words, there's nothing left to do but throw your hands in the air and surrender. In that moment, God is the only answer you need. Somehow, God is enough. Always has been, always will be."

Tammy gave herself a year off from ministry. She spent weeks and months recovering in emotional ICU. Maybe that's when her favorite verse became Psalm 34:18: "The Lord is close to the brokenhearted, and he saves those whose spirits have been crushed."[61]

But now she's moving ahead with her life task, still deeply missing Trent, but strengthened once again and touching thousands of lives for the Lord. She finds healing in laughter and joy. Some of her songs are intentionally written to dance to, because in her own words, when she's dancing, "I am moving. I am breathing. I am fighting for life. I am here, and I am trusting God."[62]

BRIEF DEBRIEF

Today's questions might stir some frightening memories or worries for you, whether you're young or old. Give yourself a break if you need it. And keep in close touch with someone you trust. (Watch for others, also, who might need to lean on you.)

- Describe a time when you've wished desperately that God, or someone, would rescue you from your pain. (Maybe right now.) How can both honesty about your pain and genuine faith in God work together in those times?

- How long did it take you to heal, if you ever did? What helped? What didn't?

- No one can escape fear and grief when enduring a loss. But brainstorm some ways you can prepare during the easier seasons of life, so you'll hang onto both God and hope when you have to ride out the hard times.

- What's the one step you will take this week to prepare for a future crisis, or to make it through one right now?

SECURE CHANNEL

Lord, when the bottom drops out and I'm in freefall, nothing makes sense. Help me connect closer with you every day, so that in those times at least *you* make sense to me. Teach me to hang onto you no matter what.

Teach me to be completely honest with you. You can handle even my most harsh and despairing thoughts. [If you need to, share your honest thoughts and feelings now.]

Come to me also with silent comfort. [If you're hurting now, you don't have to use words. Just know his presence for a while. Take as long as you need.]

I know, Lord, that [name your partners, if appropriate] are hurting and scared. Let them feel your comfort.

Background Files

To learn more about trusting God through the fear and pain, read Matthew 26:36–56; John 12:23–33; Job 1:13–22; 2:9–10; Psalm 42.

PART 4:
BE

It's coming! Some day you'll reach full maturity in Christ. You'll *arrive,* and from that point on you won't need to grow any more. No more struggles to obey. Just keep on walking close to Jesus.

Right?

Right! The day you enter heaven. Meanwhile, perfection is the goal you'll always be approaching, but never reaching in this life.

But that doesn't mean you can't reach a stage called "maturity" while you're down here. In fact, if you give yourself completely to God, you can get there soon. God wants you there. You'll be most fulfilled in life when you *get* there. Maturity is the presumed condition for Christ's followers, our natural habitat, the diet on which we thrive. Maturity is supposed to define "normal."

You'll probably discover various plateaus of maturity along your journey, enjoying a season of steady success for Jesus, then discovering another upward growth path. Unfortunately, you may also discover that it's possible to stumble off the edge. And fall a long, long way. Maintaining and enhancing spiritual maturity requires attentiveness and continual dependence on God.

Let's finish the Pray21 venture by learning about a few important principles for life as a mature Jesus-follower.

didn't you know I had to be about my Father's business?

Twelve years is a long time for any growing boy to wait. Even if he's the Messiah.

Every year at Passover time, Jesus' parents traveled several days from Nazareth to Jerusalem to celebrate the Feast. Jesus couldn't wait for his first chance to go with them later this year. Because today was the day he became a man.

It was his twelfth birthday—his coming of age, according to ancient custom. He was on his knees, committing this next stage of his life to God.

That's when the Father first spoke to him.

Hello, Son.

"Father?" He raised his eyes. Suddenly everything fell together in his mind. "Of course." He pondered silently. "Of course, Father. You've been there with me from the beginning."

Yes, Son, from the Beginning.

Jesus blinked. His stomach went cold, then warm. His mind raced with the implications.

"I've been learning the Scriptures since I could understand my parents' words. They've felt more and more like your personal letter to me. But they don't tell everything, do they?"

No. Just enough. You have a lot more to learn in the coming years, to prepare you for your mission.

Jesus trembled. "You'll guide me, right, Father?"

Absolutely. You'll do fine, Son. I love you. I'm so proud of you.

Father and Son talked a long time that morning. And every morning after that.

Including, finally, the clear winter morning when Jesus caught his first glimpse of Jerusalem. The first he could remember, anyway.

Jesus' family was traveling with relatives and friends. Along the way, his mom and dad (he privately thought of Joseph as his "earth father") had pointed out highlights of the other time they'd brought Jesus to Jerusalem—inside his mother, twelve years earlier. They even promised to show him the livestock shelter in nearby Bethlehem where they first saw his face.

Finally they topped a ridge to the north of the great city. Jesus caught his breath.

A place of destiny, Son.

Excitement flooded through Jesus, tinged with a taste of something sour, weighted with a sense of heavy responsibility. He stood taking it in for several minutes. Then ran to catch up with the caravan.

A day later, walking through the temple gates, he gazed in solemn silence at the spectacular architecture—a fitting honor for the Crafter of the universe.

That week, Jesus helped his father with the customary Passover sacrifice, pouring out his heart to his Father as the blood of the lamb poured from its veins. Jesus cried a little, trying to sort out the mix of joy (in worship) and sadness (at the price that had to be paid for Israel's sins).

The eight-day Feast ended too quickly. Now it was the evening before their departure for Nazareth. Jesus found his father, busy ensuring adequate provisions and coin for the return trip.

"Father," Jesus said from a few feet away. Joseph kept counting, his lips moving silently, his hands touching the water skins and loaves of bread. "Father…"

"What? Oh, hi, son." Joseph glanced up for a second, then went back to his preparations.

"I need to stay in Jerusalem. I must spend some time in my Father's house, tending to his business."

Joseph glanced up again. "Yeah, sure, we'll be back in our house in a few days. Meanwhile, let me take care of the business. You go play. Or go to bed."

"Yes, father." Jesus went to find his mother. His conversation with her went amazingly like that with his father. She was deep in conversation with Aunt Elizabeth and didn't want to be bothered. So Jesus went to his sleeping mat, settled down, said a few words to his Father, and slept.

Five days later, Jesus was spending his fifth day-long session in the temple courts, debating with the much-amused, much-amazed teachers of the law. He had so many questions. They had way too many answers. If Jesus had been any older, the scholars would have taken serious offense at his challenges, his embarrassing questions. But they could see that he honestly, innocently wanted to understand the Scriptures. And he had come to them, the world's experts on the subject. Their egos were soothed by his humility and respect for their authority.

Suddenly a commotion distracted them. Up ran his frantic mother, followed more slowly by his father, shaking his head.

Mary grasped him and yanked him up from his seat on the floor. "Jesus!" she screamed, tears streaking her cheeks. "Son, how could you possibly do this to us?"

Jesus stared at her—hurt, surprised, speechless.

Mary relaxed her grip, but kept hold of him, as though he might vanish. "Your father and I—we've—we've been all over Jerusalem. Searching for you. You want to kill us with worry?"

> You are Jesus' brother or sister, part of the family.

Jesus shed a tear of his own, grieved for the pain his parents had gone through. But now he was beginning to understand. He glanced at Joseph, who glared down over Mary's shoulder. "You were searching for me? But—but I told you both why I had to stay. Don't you remember? Didn't you know I had to be here, about my Father's business?"

It went right over their heads. Joseph gave Jesus a stern lecture that started in the temple court and lasted all the way to their temporary lodgings for the night—lodgings that Joseph hadn't planned into the budget. Jesus endured the scolding and said "yes sir" a lot. He meant it every time.

But after his mother had calmed down, Jesus noticed that her face was first puzzled, then thoughtful.

Back home, in the following weeks, months, and years, Jesus took every chance to attend the local synagogue in Nazareth. Gradually he was given responsibility for some of the readings, teachings, and worship. Most of his relatives, neighbors, and teachers patted him on the head and smiled as they spoke plastic placations to his parents.

But old Amos, one of the local elders, treated Jesus differently. Often he scratched his bald head and chuckled at the things that came out of Jesus' mouth. But he never mocked Jesus, even subtly. And it was he who gave Jesus the best opportunities to minister in the synagogue.[63]

"And Jesus grew in wisdom and stature, and in favor with God and men."[64]

— — —

Do you know why Jesus decided to become a human like you and me? One reason was to show us how we can be like him.

Yes, he was the one and only Messiah, and you don't get to be. But he was also God's Son, and if you've trusted Christ, you are Jesus' brother or sister, part of the family. We study Jesus' life on earth in part because he commands us to follow his example. "Anyone who claims to be intimate with God ought to live the same kind of life Jesus lived."[65] That includes the life he lived when he was twelve. And eighteen. And thirty.

Brief Debrief

Ready to live and serve like Jesus? Use your *Pray21 Journal* to record your thoughts on these questions, your prayers, your commitments. Share them with your partners, and keep on supporting each other in prayer.

- What are the traditional boundaries limiting the ways "kids" can serve in church? Which of these do you think are biblical boundaries? Which might not be?

- Can you describe one time that you or someone you know served God in an unexpected way—unexpected, maybe, because of age, abilities, personality, background, or some other pigeonhole?

- What is your Father's business?

- How does he want you to be doing it in church? Outside church?

- What's one significant new step you want to take to serve your Father?

 ### SECURE CHANNEL

Father, I'm so glad you adopted me into your family! I love you.

I'm also figuring out that you give your kids chores and household responsibilities. Some of them are fun. Some are hard. Some are dirty. Some are scary. But I want to serve you. Now.

Help me see opportunities for service that I've been overlooking. Help me accept responsibilities I've been avoiding. And if others frown on my service for you, give them insight to guide and encourage me. But give me also respect for the human authorities you've placed in my life.

I pray, too, for [name your partners], that they would give themselves wholeheartedly to your service.

BACKGROUND FILES

To learn more about conducting your Father's business, read Luke 2, especially verses 39–52; Matthew 5:1–16; 24:42–25:46; James 1:27.

won't God answer his children's persistent prayers?

"I've called to say goodbye," came the anxious voice through the phone handset. "I've got a gun to my head. I'm sorry to leave you a mess."

Randy knew his father wasn't bluffing. His hand shook as he held the phone. His stomach clenched in a knot. His face went cold with shock. He begged his father to put down the gun. Finally, in desperation, he dropped the phone, ran to his car, and drove toward his father's home.

It had all become too much for Randy's eighty-four-year-old dad. The fear, the pain, the prospect of an agonizing death. A few months earlier, he had learned that he had terminal cancer. The cancer would kill him sooner or later. But if he died tonight at his own hand, Randy knew that he would never see his unsaved father in heaven.

Heroic Measures

Randy Alcorn is a bestselling Christian author. God has used his years as a pastor, his many books, and the work of Eternal Perspective Ministries (www.epm.org) to change countless thousands of lives for Christ around the world.

But Randy grew up without Christ and without church. In high school he started to attend a church for the first time, but not to pursue God. He was chasing a girl. Fortunately, God can use ulterior motives for his purpose. He didn't miss the opportunity. He went after Randy.

In the Sunday services and the youth group, Randy heard God's good news of salvation for the first time. Soon he was reading the Bible regularly. It fascinated him. It had the ring of truth. One day, sitting in his basement, he realized that he was convinced. He believed what the Bible said about Jesus. Dropping to his knees, he confessed his sins and gave his life to Christ.

One year later, one of Randy's new life dreams came true. He led his mom to Christ.

Throughout his childhood, she had always been there for Randy. She was room mother in his classrooms, attended all his sporting events, made Christmas bright and fun every year.

Now she was with Randy in a new way, as a fellow child of God. The two of them started praying together. Their top request was Dad's salvation.

It was a tall order. If anyone had ever been utterly closed to the gospel, it was Randy's dad. Year after year he said he never wanted to hear any "religious talk." Randy's mom labored for her husband in prayer for a decade…until God relieved her from frontline duty. She went home to be with her Lord.

Randy continued to pray and to try to break through to his dad. But for twenty-two long years, all of his efforts were shut out.

Now, as Randy sped through the night, his father was eighty-four. And soon to die. Maybe already dead.

Condition Critical

Twenty minutes after his frantic phone exchange, Randy threw open the door of his dad's house. Two guns lay on the living room floor. Randy held his breath and headed for the bedroom. Just as he turned the corner, he bumped into his dad, coming out of the bedroom.

They raced to the hospital, where the doctors scheduled emergency surgery for the next morning—a surgery Randy's dad might not survive.

Before surgery, Randy walked into his father's hospital room, praying silently for his father's salvation—the latest installment in a two-decades-long conversation with God about this man he loved. His dad lay "captive" on the hospital bed. So Randy took one more opportunity. Maybe the last.

He quoted passages from Romans about our need for spiritual rescue, and the price that Christ paid on our behalf. After sharing for a half-hour, Randy asked his dad if he had ever confessed his sins and trusted Christ to save him.

"No, I haven't," was the honest reply. A pause. "But I think it's about time I did."

In the next few minutes another of Randy's life dreams came true. He prayed first. Then his father prayed aloud, asking Christ to forgive him. To Randy, it was a miracle that made the parting of the Red Sea seem small. As he walked out of that hospital room, he now knew that twenty-two years of prayer—a commitment that started in high school—had been worth every second. No matter what happened, both of his parents would some day be waiting for him in heaven.

Vitals Stabilized

Jesus once came up with a story to teach his disciples about prayer. He told about a judge who did
whatever he wanted, and didn't care what anybody

> When he hears of a need, he stops and talks to his Father about it.

thought—not even God. A widow came to him begging for protection from others who were taking advantage of her helplessness. The judge ignored her, told her to go away. But she wouldn't give up. Finally she got to be such a nuisance that he broke down and gave her what she wanted, just to get her off his back.[66]

Jesus' point? God is just the opposite of that judge—he does care about every person on earth. Including you. So if persistence made that judge grant the widow's request, how much more willing is your loving Father to respond to your persistent prayers? Don't ever give up!

In Jesus' own words: "What makes you think God won't step in and work justice for his chosen people, who continue to cry out for help? Won't he stick up for them? I assure you, he will. He will not drag his feet. But how much of that kind of persistent faith will the Son of Man find on the earth when he returns?"[67]

Randy will tell you that he's always found it hard to spend long periods of time in prayer. But he's come to realize that conversation with God isn't a one-size-fits-all arrangement. His walk with God has become a pattern of brief prayer breaks throughout the day, accompanied by a constant sense of dependence on God. When he hears of a need, he stops and talks to his Father about it. He asks God to help him see prayer as an adventure in which he enters God's presence and meets him face to face. He prays to become so absorbed with God that he wouldn't want to do anything else.

And that's what God has given him, sometimes. Randy wants more.

By the way, remember that girl who motivated Randy to walk through a church door? Her name was Nanci, and now she's his wife and favorite prayer partner.

Complete Recovery

Randy's father survived the surgery, and he lived five more years. Eventually the family knew that his homecoming would be soon. They were gathered one April day around his bed, and Randy read aloud from the book of Revelation.

He was nearing the end of the Bible's last chapter: "The Spirit and the bride say, 'Come!' And let him who hears say, 'Come!' Whoever is thirsty, let him come; and whoever wishes, let him take the free gift of the water of life."[68] In that moment, his father released a breath. And didn't take another.

Randy was filled with grief. And joy. The grief is healing. The joy will never end.

BRIEF DEBRIEF

As you journal your responses to the following questions, let the process be a conversation with God. Tell him your thoughts and feelings, and open up to his guidance and love. Open up to your partners, too. Help each other develop more solid and enjoyable prayer habits.

- When you pray, do you think God is listening? Do you think he cares about your requests? Why or why not?

- There are a variety of ways to communicate with God. Take a minute and brainstorm creatively about ways that might work best for you. (Think about all the ways people communicate— speaking, writing, body language, art, music, actions, and more. How might you use these for relating to God?)

- What are a couple of God-honoring desires you want more than anything else?

- What is your strategy for bringing these requests regularly to God? What is your first step?

Secure Channel

Lord, you're always there. Amazing! And you're better than hanging out with a movie star or sports hero. You can do anything, you know everything, and you never stop loving me. So why don't I connect with you more?

I want to.

I will.

Create in my heart a hunger to be with you. Help me be patient for that hunger to grow, so I don't give up when prayer doesn't come easy.

Do the same thing for [name your partners]. Give them more and more joy in your presence every day.

Background Files

To learn more about the realities behind Randy's prayer venture, read Luke 11:1–13; 18:1–8; Ephesians 6:18; Philippians 4:6–7; 1 Thessalonians 5:17.

do you put a lamp under the bed?

Rachael was thirteen when doctors told her that cancer would take her life within eight weeks. A friend of the family called to encourage her, but Rachael was already one step ahead. She asked, "Would you pray that, before I die, I can share Jesus with my entire high school?"

Her dying wish—what she wanted more than anything else—was not something for herself, but something for others. She cared more about the dawn of heaven for others than her own earthly sunset. Rachael saw her limited time on earth in the light of an unlimited eternal forever. She was committed to representing her King, sharing his truth—despite her circumstances.

The doctors gave Rachael eight weeks, but God gave Rachael three years to fulfill her mission—to speak and live for him on her high school campus. Sure, she was scared. And she had her questions and weak moments. Who wouldn't? But her genuine humanness made her all the more credible. Her cancer gave her a unique voice, and no one at her school could ignore it. Her teachers and fellow students couldn't understand why this dying girl felt so sorry for them. She should be feeling sorry for herself.

From a human perspective her circumstances seemed hopeless. What better time to shine for God!

On her sixteenth birthday, Rachael announced, "I'm ready to go home to be with the Lord. I've finished what he sent me here to do."

She made a special request of her high school principal. She asked that the entire student body be allowed to attend her memorial service. God had been working in his heart; he said yes.

Rachael's mission on earth came to a close. She finally went Home.

On the day set aside for her memory and honor, the principal made buses available during school hours for anyone who wanted to attend Rachael's memorial service. Busloads of teens from all kinds of backgrounds got off those buses and entered that church. Eggheads sat next to dope heads. The building was packed out. And her pastor read a letter she had written for this occasion:

> *Dear friends,*
> *Please do not be sad for me today, for I am in a place where there is no more sickness, no more death, and no more tears. I am in heaven, and my prayer for you is that I will see you here someday and we will share eternity. My Savior Jesus Christ has made a way for you to get here… Love, Rachael*

When the pastor finished reading Rachael's letter, he invited people to come forward and ask Jesus into their hearts. Hundreds got up from their seats, walked to the front of the church, kneeled by Rachael's casket, and received the crown of life.

Jesus once asked, "Does anyone bring a lamp home and put it under a washtub or beneath the bed? Don't you put it up on a table or on the mantel?"[69] The answer's obvious, right? Especially for God's people, here on a lifelong rescue mission. So then, why do so many of us—*children of God, the brilliantly shining lights of the world*—keep ourselves safely sealed up in light-proof boxes? Our heart-piercing, life-changing rays stop one foot from our faces, squelched by lead-lined walls.

Rachael chose to hold high her 10,000-watt halogen, visible to all, as she walked the halls of her school. And people saw Jesus.

Jesus also once said, "Unless a kernel of wheat is planted in the soil and dies, it remains alone. But its death will produce many new kernels—a plentiful harvest of new lives."[70] In Rachael's case, she didn't die *in order* to save others. Physically, her body would have died anyway, no matter how she used her remaining time. But long before her spirit left her body, she served others by dying in a different way. She voluntarily died to a bunch of things that most of us cling onto…with a death grip… for dear life.

> Hold your light high! And don't be afraid to die a little.

Rachael died to self-pity. Have you performed a funeral for yours? Buried it deep?

Rachael died to self-centeredness. Can you point to your tombstone?

Rachael died to self-indulgence. Do you think it's time to euthanize?

And who even needs any of those self-attitudes? Think about it. They're me-leeches, not me-boosters.

Rachael died to self…and found Rachael-in-Christ—genuine, adventurous, free, full of life, purposeful, satisfied, at peace, happy.

What did she lose? Nothing real.

What did she gain? Everything real.

And in so gaining, she also helped hundreds of other people find everything that's real. Maybe ultimately thousands. How many of those students went home and told their parents about Jesus? How many will become fully devoted followers of Christ—spiritual leaders in their homes, pastors, teachers, or evangelists?

Death isn't the end for the Lord's messengers, children of Royalty, and Rachael lived out that truth as her high school watched. "God can do anything…far more than you could ever imagine or guess or request in your wildest dreams!"[71] That's what he did in Rachael's life. One of God's kids had cancer, and she led hundreds of people to her Father.

The way we live today determines the legacy we will leave behind us.

Hold your light high!

And don't be afraid to die a little. [72]

BRIEF DEBRIEF

Here are a few more questions and challenges for you to weigh in your heart—questions and challenges for Christ-followers of all ages. Record your responses in your *Pray21 Journal*. Process them and pray about them with others, toward personalized commitments and real-life follow-through.

- Think about your life on earth so far. What will you be remembered for when you're gone? What will people say at your funeral?

- What have you contributed to the lives of those around you? How are they different because you lived?

- What's one simple but stretching step you will take this week to shine God's love and truth into the lives of others?

- What has to die in order for this to happen?

- What support or resources do you need from others this week? What do they need from you?

Secure Channel

Lord, you've given me eternal light and life. What an amazing gift! Thank you.

As grateful as I am, though, I know I've sometimes kept this light to myself, while you want me to shine it and share it. I'm sorry for the opportunities I've missed…the people I've left in the dark. Please forgive me.

I want to start, right now, burning brightly and boldly into the darkness of this world. Give me courage to climb out from under the bed. Help me die to the fear of what others think. Show me how to live as royalty-on-assignment, the child of the King who wants the whole world to be in his family.

I pray this, too, for [name your partners], that they would be able to put to death their self-attitudes, drop the walls, and shine you to people around them.

Background Files

To learn more about what Rachael knew and how you can shine as God's light in your world, read Mark 4:1–34; John 12:23–30; Matthew 5:14–16.

do you really love me?

Sheri started praying for and with her son Jake from the time he was two. She prayed especially that Jake would see for himself the hand of God at work in his life. No second-hand faith for her son. Sure enough, Jake cultivated a personal passion for God and for prayer.

The family lives in a small town in Central Oregon. The nearest real mall is four hours away in Portland. When Jake was thirteen, he and his mom planned a rare shopping spree in Portland, to spend a year's savings. About this time, Sheri was praying for Jake to learn to see giving as a joy and a privilege. But buying nice things with honest money is good, too. So off they went.

As they drove, they made yet another request—that God would give them a divine appointment.

God wasted no time.

At the mall, Jake headed for the computer store. Sheri was following when she noticed a teenage girl curled up on an outdoor bench, shaking, coatless in the freezing weather. She was obviously in pain—physically and emotionally. Sheri couldn't help herself. She went up and said, "Please let me pray for you."

The girl scowled. *"Whatever,"* was her sarcastic response.

Sheri was shocked, but stubborn. "I'm not leaving until I pray for you."

Angrily, the girl gave in. "Go ahead and get it over with."

Jake walked up just as Sheri began: "Dear God, I don't know what this girl has been through, but you do. Please let her know you love her and that you can and will help her. Please show her today, somehow, that you see her broken heart and you can restore all she has lost. In Jesus' name I pray, amen."

In that second, the ice dam broke, melted into tears. The girl started crying uncontrollably, telling her story between sobs. Kendra (we'll call her) had gotten pregnant. Her parents told her to abort the baby, but she wanted to keep it and marry her boyfriend—the baby's father. (Let's call him Shawn.) So her parents kicked her out on the streets. Kendra and Shawn kept the baby, slept under a bridge, and still went to high school. But that was no life for a baby, so they gave it up for adoption.

While Kendra was talking, Shawn walked up. And when she had finished, Jake said, "Mom, it's time to shop."

Sheri looked at her son in surprise. "Jake, did you hear their situation?"

"Yes," he said. "That's why we need to spend our shopping money on them."

That day Jake took Shawn and bought him clothes, a sleeping bag, shoes, and a backpack. Sheri did the same for Kendra. As they were about to part ways, God answered one more prayer. A prayer that the young couple prayed—the prayer for forgiveness and new life in Christ.

Later, the ministry of which Jake's family was a part paid for an apartment for the couple.

That morning, Jake had envisioned riding home with shopping bags covering the back seat. The back seat stayed empty. But Jake was full to the brim. Spilling over.

"Mom," he said, "that was the best day I've ever had!"

At first glance—even at fifth or sixth glance—Kendra and Shawn wouldn't seem the type that good Christians would hang out with. Ragged, dirty, resentful. Their first reaction to kindness was spite. They came from a foreign life history. And besides, the couple's problems weren't Sheri's or Jake's fault. Most of us would understand if Sheri and Jake had simply passed by, asking God to send someone who could identify better with the girl, then feeling good about showing the love of God, as they did their shopping.

But they'd be demonstrating that they didn't really love Jesus Christ.

Once a Jewish Old Testament expert approached Jesus. He was a good Jew who lived God's law to a *tav* (that's a Hebrew *T*). The legal genius decided to embarrass Jesus. "Teacher," he said with mock respect, "how do I get eternal life?"

Jesus smiled and invited the man to answer his own question, from the Scriptures.

Aha! His chance to shine. The scholar stood straight, cleared his throat, and quoted two passages: "Love the Lord your God with everything in you" and "Love your neighbor just the way you love yourself." (Notice the connection here between loving God and loving people. It'll be on the test later.)

The man was taken aback by Jesus' applause. "Bravo!" said the Messiah. "Perfect answer."

Then in a sober but caring tone, Jesus said, "Obey both of those, and you'll live forever."

Suddenly the law expert started to remember one or two times he had behaved unlovingly toward others. He was worried. Then he thought of a loophole. "But, teacher, not everyone is my neighbor. Certainly not the Gentiles, or the sinners. Define 'neighbor.'"

"Happy to," answered Jesus. And he told a story. A Jewish man was traveling alone when he was robbed, stripped, horribly beaten, and left for dead. Along came a holy man—one of the righteous leaders of Israel, teacher of God's love. He saw the broken, bloody man, but kept as much distance as possible as he passed. A second holy man traveled by and did the same.

Then came the most repulsive kind of person in the Jewish imagination. A mixed-blood, idolatrous neighbor of Israel. A Samaritan. Not the type that good Jews would hang out with. Morally filthy, natural enemies. Foreign in the extreme. And besides, the poor man's problems weren't the Samaritan's fault. Any Jew would understand if the Samaritan had passed by, wished a pious blessing on the man, then continued his journey, feeling he'd done the best that could be expected.

Any Jew would be shocked. The Samaritan's heart broke. He used his meager supplies to treat and bandage the man's wounds. He put his arms around the man and helped him to his feet, then onto his donkey. He led the donkey to an inn, paid for a room, and cared for the unfortunate Jew throughout the night. The next morning he paid for several more days and instructed the innkeeper, "Spare no expense. Give him whatever he needs. I'll be back, and I'll cover the tab."

Jesus paused to make sure the law expert was following. Then he said, "Now, I'd like *you* to define 'neighbor.' Which of the three travelers was a neighbor to the beaten man?"

The scholar glanced around, swallowed, and said, "The Samar— Uh, the one who had mercy on him."

"Good answer," said Jesus. "You go and do the same."[73]

Love them all. And not just with a prayer and a smile, but with your life.

Important point: The lawyer was right to connect loving God with loving people. In fact, Jesus made the same connection once with his young disciple, Peter. Three times Jesus asked, "Peter, do you really love me?" Three times Peter answered, "Absolutely, Lord." And three times Jesus answered Peter's answer with "Then take care of my sheep."[74]

In other words, "Peter, if you really love me, take care of those I love—all of them. The beautiful and the ugly. The lost and the found. The nice and the hateful. Those you click with and those you don't. Love them all. And not just with a prayer and a smile, but with your life. That's how you really love me."

Outside a mall in Portland, Oregon, a thirteen-year-old named Jake knew how to love Jesus.[75]

BRIEF DEBRIEF

Try to let God's heart fill yours as you consider these questions and journal your responses. Pray for your own inner change, and for change in your partners. Help each other live out a genuine love. We all need help, no matter how old or how accomplished.

- What kind of people do you have the hardest time loving? Why do you think this is?

- Talk about God's attitude toward those same people. Try to get inside his heart and see through his eyes. Try to imagine how he honestly feels toward them. Does it help your attitude?

- What is one opportunity in your daily life to do something kind for an "unlovable" person?

- The mere doing is good and loving, but how can you cultivate a heart that honestly wants to?

- What's your first step?

SECURE CHANNEL

No, Lord, not him. Please don't ask me to love her.

Okay, I've been honest. That's how I feel. (Forgive me.) Now change me. I want to love everyone you love. I want to love the way you love, for the reasons you love. I want to love no matter what.

And I want to love with action. Show me how. Give me courage. Help me get over myself, my fears, and my pride. Help me do miracles in a life that needs you.

Please also help [name your partners] to love all kinds of people in their lives. Fill them with your heart, with your sight, with your touch of healing love.

BACKGROUND FILES

To learn more about loving Jesus by loving people, read Luke 6:27–38; 10:25–37; John 21:1–17.

are you able to drink from the same cup as me?

One day Mrs. Zebedee, the mother of James and John, came to Jesus and asked that her sons be seated in the places of greatest honor in his kingdom, to the right and left of his throne.

Jesus could have chewed her out (and the boys) for being arrogant. But instead he took them seriously and asked, "Are you capable of drinking the cup that I'm about to drink?"[76] In other words, "Will you follow me through suffering and death?"

They said yes. Jesus watched their faces, then said, "As a matter of fact, you will." He smiled kindly. "But as for who gets which seats, that's up to my Father. Sorry."[77]

Later, the night before Jesus died, he stripped down like a slave and washed his disciples' stinking feet. When he was finished, he asked, "Do you understand what I've just done? I'm the important one. But I washed your feet. That's how I want you to treat each other."[78]

The following stories are by young people involved with Brother Andrew's Open Doors ministry, helping persecuted Christians around the world. Watch for several examples of ordinary people serving humbly, as Jesus did, and drinking from the cup of Christ's suffering.

--- --- ---

I never realized a TV program would change the rest of my life. The program was "The Dying Rooms," and it showed the horrific conditions of orphanages in China, where thousands of abandoned children live and die. As a family we couldn't just watch this and do nothing. After years of prayer, paperwork, stress, and excitement, we adopted my two Chinese sisters.

I started to pray regularly for China and to learn the language. At a Christian youth festival called "Soul Survivor," I was challenged to reach out to those in need overseas. I contacted Open Doors because I knew they had many projects in China. The youth program, Student Underground, was soon to be launched, and I was asked whether I'd like to be more involved.

At first I was just on the mailing list. This changed when I read an article by Brother Andrew. He wrote: "But we won't see a demonstration of this power [of Christ's resurrection] unless we combine it with every effort to meet the needs of those of the Body of Christ who suffer for their faith. I believe that if we don't have that love—that willingness to share and suffer—then we don't know God (1 John 4:8). It is so clear. The persecuted church cannot make it without us (Hebrews 11:40). Neither can we make it without them." I had to do something more. Initially it was writing to those who suffer for their faith, writing to governments campaigning on their behalf, giving, and praying for the persecuted church at my school prayer group. Things grew, and I became a networker for my area, organizing activities such as a Shockwave event.

Shockwave was a worldwide prayer event in which young people across the world held half nights of prayer for the persecuted church, from 7 P.M. until midnight, so the prayer moved with the time zones and twenty-four hours were covered. With a couple of my friends, I organized an event in our town. It was a big step of faith, and I was really scared. My fears were unfounded, though, and we had a fantastic night of productive prayer.

Recently I read the story of a seventeen-year-old girl in Asia who was martyred because she refused to deny Jesus, and God seemed to ask me if I would be willing to give up my life in the same situation. It was no coincidence that later that evening I was reading Philippians 1:21, where Paul writes, "For to me, to live is Christ and to die is gain."

Over the years I've felt God calling me to work in China. Exactly

*what God wants me to do there, I don't know, I just want to do
something that will bring others to Christ and glory to God.*

—Beth, 15, United Kingdom[79]

– – –

*On one of our first trips into China, my teammate Dale and I were
given instructions to wait the next morning outside our hotel for a
white van to pick us up and drive us a few hours north to a drop-
off point. We were to leave the [smuggled] Bibles there and take
a plane back to Hong Kong. The instructions were vague; we were
to be outside at 7:30 A.M. sharp, but we were never told what time
we would be picked up, where we were going, or whom we would
be meeting. But after spending the night praying, we both felt at
peace, knowing that God was in complete control.*

*We paced around the hotel driveway for two hours before a van
pulled up. Inside, an entire Chinese family greeted us with hand-
shakes and head tapping (which we later learned was their way of
blessing us). We soon found out that none of them spoke English.
We don't speak Chinese. The only way we could communicate was
through very simple sign language and lots of smiles, and by trusting that God's presence in our lives would act as our translator.*

*The drive was surprising. The family fed us the entire way, with a
variety of food, from warm Pepsi to salted eggs. They gladly shared a
week's worth of food with us. We even stopped at a roadside market
where they bought fried chicken feet for us. At first I was skeptical
about eating the food, but the trip coordinators had said that not
eating the offered food would be very offensive, even if it was food
we were allergic to or didn't like. So we ate everything, even the
chicken feet. And we smiled while choking it down, knowing that we
were being served by our brothers and sisters in Christ.*

*After seven hours in a rickety van, we arrived at the Xiemen
airport. The mother and daughter walked us to the ticket counter
and bought us two tickets to Shen Zhen. Then they turned to*

us, waved, got back in the van, and drove off. Dale and I were left staring, wondering what was next. We sat for another three hours, considering what our role was and how we were used. At first glance, it seemed as if we had just taken a day trip into China, turned around, and come back. But we realized that we were being used to escort the Bibles through a difficult area of mainland China. Our presence ensured that the family took no responsibility for the Bibles if we happened to be stopped by police. We were made pawns, and I can't imagine a greater way to be used by God.

Dale and I had no great heroic part to play. Nothing depended on our strengths or spiritual gifts. Our role was to sit in a van for seven hours and smile. There are no small roles in furthering God's kingdom. Sometimes the most we can do is to let go of what we know we can do and allow God to just use our lives. Submitting to his hand in all times is difficult, but we know he is sovereign and that his plan for us is perfect. Even if it involves chicken feet.

—Sarah, 23, California[80]

BRIEF DEBRIEF

Jesus is speaking to followers of all ages and abilities. Listen and share your heart honestly with him and others as you weigh his challenge. Record your responses to these questions in your *Pray21 Journal*.

- Jesus asks you the question he asked James and John: "Are you able to drink the same cup I drank?" What's your honest answer at this moment? If you're not happy with that answer, what might help you change it?

- Jesus might some day ask you to suffer physically for him. But what are other ways he's likely to ask you to serve and suffer for him?

- What step of service or sacrifice is he asking you to take now?

- How will you start?

SECURE CHANNEL

Lord, I'm scared. But so were you. I guess you understand.
You've promised that your followers will face suffering
for your name, but you also promised strength, victory, and great reward.[81]
Help me keep my eyes on you, so that any humiliation or sacrifice seems
small compared to you.

Also give [name your partners] courage and eagerness to serve and
suffer for you.

BACKGROUND FILES

To learn more about serving and suffering for Jesus,
read Matthew 20:20–23; John 13:1–17; Philippians 1:12–21; 2:1–18.

will you really die for me?

Simon Peter…fisher of fish, fisher of men, bestselling author, and renowned church leader. You may have read his writings in the popular anthology commonly known as *The Book*, which also includes works by such historic authors as Moses, David, Isaiah, John, and, of course, the apostle Paul. Our *Time Travel Review* reporter caught up with Simon Peter in the year AD 63, at a home on the outskirts of Nero's Rome. He was happy to talk about experiences that led to his two books, *Peter's Letter* and *Peter's Letter II: The Sequel.*

Time Travel Review: Now, Simon… Do you mind if I call you Simon?

Simon Peter: I prefer Peter. It's the nickname Jesus gave me.

TTR: And the significance behind the nickname?

SP: Oh (laughs), that goes way back. As you can see, I've always been a teeny tiny little fella… (indicates his huge frame). My ego used to be as big as my body. Bigger. That meant I could lead, and I could be stubborn about good things. But it got me in trouble sometimes— stubborn about the wrong things. Anyway, Jesus always teased me about my size and my boulder-like personality. So one day he said, "Simon, I have the perfect name for you. You're now Peter, the Rock." Just a joke at first. But it stuck.[82]

TTR: Sounds like you and Jesus were pretty close.

SP: Oh, sure. James and John and me, we were his best friends. He let us come the time he raised the little girl from the dead. We were there when Moses and Elijah showed up, on the mountain, and Jesus was transfigured. And…well…he took us three with him to pray…um…the night before he died.[83]

TTR: You seem uncomfortable talking about that night.

SP: It wasn't one of my better days.

TTR: Mind filling us in?

SP: (Long pause.) Okay. Might help your readers. Especially if they love God, they're going strong for him, hauling in the big catches. And then they blow it big. They fail God. That was me… (tears up, voice quavers). I never thought… (deep breath).

See, in those last weeks, Jesus started saying some scary things. Telling us he'd be crucified, and other crazy things. I kept trying to get him to stop. Boy, did he get on my case. Called me Satan. (Winces.) I had it coming. So, by Passover evening, we were all nervous. All his talk about betrayal, dying, going away. I thought a positive word would help, so I said, "Lord, I'll die with you. If I have to." Thought it might cheer him up. He gave me one of his sad, disappointed looks and said, "Will you really die for me?" He said I was going to disown him that very night. Three times.[84]

TTR: And was he right?

SP: (Softly.) Sorry to say…he was. He got himself arrested, see, just like he'd been saying. Then we disciples, we scattered like a school of fish. But I stopped and followed Jesus and the guards to the high priest's place. I tried to be inconspicuous with the crowd outside, but my accent gave me away as a northerner, like Jesus. Then someone recognized me. Yeah, Jesus was right. I denied him, three times. I'll never forget that rooster call. "Traitor! Traitor!" After that is a blur. I thought about killing myself, like Judas. I was really in bad shape.[85]

TTR: So you failed Jesus so badly that you felt disqualified to serve him?

SP: You bet your fish bait, I was disqualified. Not just "felt." I really was. Loser with a capital LOO. And a capital ZER, too. I was sure I'd bought my ticket to hell.

TTR: And yet, here you are, serving him in the capital of the Roman Empire. You headed up First Church of Earth, in Jerusalem. Spread the gospel through Asia.

SP: No credit of mine. Only by the incredible, awesome, unbelievable, infinite—I could keep adding words forever—only by the incredible grace of God.

TTR: Tell us about when you first realized you were still on Jesus' staff.

SP: Well, y'see, by then we knew Jesus was alive. I saw his empty tomb. I saw him, touched him, talked to him. And one night seven of us were up home by Lake Galilee, all restless and antsy, and I thought fishing was as good an idea as any. So we went. But "no luck on the lake," as we used to say. The sun came up, and we were out in the boat, throwing the nets, dragging them in. Nothing. Then someone on shore said, "Throw the net on the right-hand side." That made me mad. We were experts, and nobody was going to… Well, we did it. And the boat almost sank from the load. John caught on first. "It's the Lord," he said.

Now, I don't always think when I get excited, and I went and jumped in the water, to get to Jesus. (Laughs.) He had a nice breakfast ready, and we all ate together like old times. Then Jesus got me by myself. "Simon son of John," he said, "do you love me?" He asked me three times. Just… Just like I disowned him three times. Of course I loved him. Said so. Three times. And each time he said, "Take care of my sheep."

But I knew he was saying, "That's right, Peter, you hurt me bad. But I didn't give up on you. So don't give up on yourself. You're forgiven. I want you on my crew." (Tears up again.)[86]

TTR: That was very important for you.

SP: (Suddenly animated.) Jesus…and doing his will…that's my life. He's why I breathe and walk and talk and…and…*everything!* To lose that… (shakes his head, at a loss for words). Then finding out he could pull me up from drowning and put me right back in the boat—I've never felt any bigger relief in my life.

TTR: What did Jesus mean, "Take care of my sheep"?

SP: That's the rest of my story. Turns out, Jesus has a lot of "sheep" out there in the world. And we need to find them, lead them to the Shepherd, and care for them. First we received the Holy Spirit on Pentecost. Nothing could've happened without him. And that day I got to preach about Jesus. And three thousand people became Jesus-followers! God used a torn, tangled net like *me* to pull in those souls. What a rush!

I testified in front of the Jewish leaders. I was jailed and beaten. I took the gospel to the first Gentiles—y'know, the folks that aren't Jews?[87]

TTR: I'm familiar with the term.

SP: My life didn't go perfect. But I had way more keepers than throwbacks.

TTR: And you have two bestselling books to your credit.

SP: Well, it's kind of silly calling a couple of letters "books." But, yeah, they've been big hits. That's because it was God who really wrote them.[88]

TTR: Oh, you had a ghostwriter.

SP: (Laughs.) That's right, a *Holy* Ghost.

TTR: Um, yes. Well, Simon Peter—

SP: Just Peter.

TTR: Peter, it's been so good to chat. On behalf of our readers—especially those who identify with your mistakes—thank you for being so open.

SP: All part of the mission.

BRIEF DEBRIEF

Work through these questions prayerfully with your forgiving, accepting Father. And let your words and prayers with your partners be God's expressions of forgiveness to each other.

- How big a deal does the idea of failing Jesus seem to you? Explain your answer.

- What does Jesus honestly think and feel about the times you fail him?

- What's the way of dealing with your failures that makes Jesus happiest?

- Can you think of a past or present failure that still has you down, out of God's game?

- How will you confront that failure, and get back on with the mission?

SECURE CHANNEL

Lord, when I've failed you, I start to think you don't want me back. I honestly believe, then, that I'm helping you by staying away.

But you tell me you want me back every time. No matter what I've done. Give me honesty to admit my sins and mistakes. Give me strength to accept any negative consequences I've caused. Then show me your unlimited forgiveness—let me honestly believe it. And point me back to the next job you have for me.

Do the same for [name your partners] as they deal with their haunting failures. [Be specific if you can.]

BACKGROUND FILES

To learn more about getting back in the boat after failure, read John 13:36–38; 18:1–27; 21:1–23; Acts 2:1–47; Galatians 2:11–21.

three-week
checkpoint

In some ways the last three weeks have been a real-life challenge. You've grown, and maybe you've engaged in a spiritual battle or two. You've probably started living out some new principles in your daily life and ministry. That's great. That's real. That's living for God here and now.

But also, in some ways these 21 days have been the conditioning workout for the main event—the rest of your life. You've been making decisions that you still need to put into practice. Clarifying God's game plan for you for the next few months…or years, or decades. Laying some of the blacktop that paves the road to your divine purpose and destiny.

Welcome to the finish line. Welcome to the starting gate.

In Part 4 of your Pray21 venture, you've been challenged to *Be*. To be about your Father's business on earth, now. To be persistent in prayer. To be a light shining in the darkness. To be a lover and caretaker of all kinds of people. To be a servant, and sometimes to be a fellow-sufferer with Christ. To be quick to admit your failures and get back on task for God.

Be.

These are a few of the basics of lifelong, mature commitment to Christ. They're the habits that will help you see your path more clearly as you go. They'll give you the wisdom and stamina and heart to carry out your mission.

And don't forget—*you're on the job now*, even though you may not have finished reading God's job description for you. Take the assignments God sends. Some will come to you, and some you'll need to go find.

And pray. Together and alone. All the time.

Remember, this exercise is for participants of all ages. We're all on the journey.

Prayerfully plan with God and your partners, looking ahead to the next couple of months. That's the time frame that it may take to establish habitual obedience in the three areas of commitment you're choosing out of this venture. Journal your thoughts as you choose your third goal, as you get ready to launch into Pray22. And Pray23. And Pray24…

1. As best you can right now, finish this sentence: *I think the mission to which God is calling me is…* (Stay open to mission clarification or reassignment later.)

2. What is one specific ministry opportunity you want to pursue as part of this mission? Something you're already doing, or something new? Something boldly visible, or making a difference behind the scenes? Pouring all of yourself into one activity, or touching several causes, each in a significant way? Don't be afraid to dream.

3. From the topics and challenges of this third week (Days 15–21), choose your third new step of growth and obedience. It could be something new, or turning up the dial on a goal you've already been pursuing. Or it might come from your "leftover" dream goals listed under Question 7 in the One-Week or the Two-Week Checkpoints.

4. **Rubber Meets the Road:** Write down your specific plan for follow-through. Will this commitment stretch you? Is it reachable for you? How will you measure success for this goal?

5. **Rubber Meets the Road:** Take out your schedules, PDAs, Blackberries…or even just that napkin over there. Set specific dates, times, and places for at least weekly progress check-ins with each other. Meeting in person is best, but phone is good. Set appointments for at least the next eight weeks.

6. Write down any other growth areas or commitments from Days 15–21 that you would like to pursue some day. (Idea: Put reminders to yourself in your schedule to look back at these ideas once each month. Regularly reevaluate your current goals, and adjust as needed.)

Another Word from Timothy

Remember at the beginning of this book, I said, "If you've placed your faith in Christ, you can know with absolute certainty who you are"? Have you achieved that knowledge? That certainty?

For 21 days you've been on a journey of discovery. You've read. Pondered. Prayed. Talked. Jesus-follower, do you know who you are?

You're a child of the King. Born for greatness. Destined to bring God glory. Your birth Father is the King to whom all other kings, emperors, presidents, and dictators must bow. You have rights. Privileges. He has plans for you. Believe it. Never let go of it.

So what's next? Well, it could be many things. But as you continue with discovery, my final word to you is a warning: Someone wants to rob you. An enemy waits in the wings. You know he's a liar, but he's very good at it. He's looking to confuse you about your identity, to poison your relationship with Jesus.

Stop him at all costs.

Ever since Eden, men and women have battled him. And lost. Relied on mere human logic. Gave up on faith, or never tried it. What birthrights were ours! What a position of honor. All gone.

Great news: What Adam and Eve abandoned, Jesus Christ restored. And, son or daughter of God, that *can't* be taken away from you. Once a prince or princess of heaven, always a prince or princess. You've always been a warrior; now you're assured victory.

The marks of your heritage are permanently tattooed on your heart. Confidence. Courage. Hope. Belief. Faith. Trust. Let them show. These are the Bill of Rights for God's anointed. That's you!

Now, on your enemy's hit list, right next to your name, are your prayer partners. Stay in contact. Remind them of their significance. Replace the words of doubt with God's Word of truth. The truth won't always seem reasonable. What feels right has nothing to do with who you are. Tell each other. Often. Don't let the lies take root.

And dream. With God, many "castles in the sky" are *not* hallucinations. The hope God has placed in you—to change your life and your world—

begins when you change your mind. Believe in who you are. Your new, God-transplanted heart knows. Trust its true, deepest confidences.[89] When someone asks you, "Just who do you think you are?"—whip out your ID card: "Child of the King."

For millennia, God has had a task prepared for you. And he's prepared you for the task. He created you with the right raw material, and he's been refining and shaping you. The renovation continues; you're still growing. But it's time to get on with the dream. Chase it down with confident certainty. God is birthing the dream in your heart. And since it's his dream, that means it—or something it's becoming—is destined to come true. You *will* live the dream. Your inner vision will become visible to others on the outside, where God's glory is revealed.

The second-century church father Irenaeus said it well: "The glory of God is man fully alive." Don't let the enemy keep you partly dead. His one purpose is to keep you from fulfilling yours.[90] With Jesus, you'll win.

Your mission, should you choose to accept it, begins now.

And this is one message that will never self-destruct.

(Endnotes)

1 See John 6:1–17; Mark 6:7–13, 30–45; 8:1–10.

2 See Acts 8.

3 Matthew 20:32, NLT.

4 See Luke 13:18–21.

5 Matthew 9:28.

6 See John 9.

7 The language in this and the following quote are slightly updated to contemporary English.

8 See Matthew 14:22–33.

9 See the book of Esther in the Old Testament.

10 See Psalm 139:5.

11 See Luke 23:33–34.

12 See John 14:9.

13 See Matthew 25:31–46.

14 Most of this information is from the Ruby Bridges Foundation website (www.rubybridges.org).

15 John 3:16, NLT.

16 Ephesians 1:4, NLT.

17 Psalm 139:13–16.

18 Matthew 10:29–31, NLT.

19 John 6:70.

20 John 14:1–3.

21 John 15:18–19, 21, NLT.

22 John 16:33.

23 Matthew 16:27, NIV.

24 Mark 8:35, NLT.

25 John 14:6, NLT.

26 Matthew 10:32, 38, NLT.

27 Matthew 12:48, 50.

28 Matthew 13:8, NLT.

29 Matthew 10:34–35.

30 Rosa's letter taken from "Sowing God's Word" in Jesus Freaks Vol II, by dc Talk and the Voice of the Martyrs (Minneapolis, MN: Bethany House, 2002), 87–88. Bethany House is a division of Baker Publishing Group.

31 Mark 8:34, 36–37, NLT.

32 See Colossians 1:13.

33 Luke 5:23–24.

34 See Luke 5:17–26.

35 "A Total Life Change" in Encounters with God, compiled by Kelly Carr (Cincinnati: Standard Publishing, 2005), 131–5. Used by permission.

36 See 1 John 1:9; Hebrews 10:17–18.

37 See Psalm 34:18; 147:3; Isaiah 61:1–3.

38 See John 9:1–3, 6–7; 2 Corinthians 12:7–10.

39 See Luke 7:36–50.

40 John 1:38.

41 See Genesis 2:16–17; 3:1–24.

42 See Genesis 6–7.

43 See Matthew 26:14–16, 46–50; 27:1–5; quoted Scripture: Proverbs 22:6.

44 Romans 1:20.

45 Romans 2:14–15.

46 Mark 4:23, NLT; see also Matthew 11:15; 13:9, 43; Mark 4:9; Luke 8:8; 14:35.

47 1 Samuel 3:9.

48 1 Samuel 3:10.

49 Read Samuel's story in 1 Samuel 1–4, 7, 9–10, 13, 15–16.

50 Matthew 16:15–16.

51 John 18:4–5.

52 See John 18:5–6; Exodus 3:13–14.

53 Main sources for Al's story: <www.bossthemovement.com>, <www.aldelano.com>. Also consulted: David Kithcart, "Al Hollingsworth: Who's the Real Boss?" <http://www.cbn.com/700club/features/amazing/Al_Hollingsworth051007.aspx>; Doug Trouten, "The Boss with the Big Heart" <http://www.charismamag.com/display.php?id=8485>.

54 See John 14:6.

55 See Luke 22:44.

56 Matthew 26:38, NLT.

57 See Matthew 26:39, 42.

58 Matthew 26:39, NLT.

59 John 12:27–28.

60 John 12:31–32.

61 NCV.

62 Portions of Tammy's story adapted from her biography on her website (http://www.tammytrent.com/bio.html).

63 See Luke 2, especially verses 39–51.

64 Luke 2:52, NIV.

65 1 John 2:6.

66 See Luke 18:1–8.

67 Luke 18:7–8.

68 Revelation 22:17, NIV.

69 Mark 4:21.

70 John 12:24, NLT.

71 Ephesians 3:20.

72 Rachael's story adapted from *My Prince Will Come: Waiting for the Lord's Return* © 2005 by Sheri Rose Shepherd.

73 See Luke 10:25–37.

74 See John 21:15–17.

75 Adapted from *Preparing Him for the Other Woman* © 2006 by Sheri Rose Shepherd.

76 Matthew 20:22.

77 See Matthew 20:20–23.

78 See John 13:1–17.

79 Adapted from Brother Andrew with Verne Becker, *The Calling* (Grand Rapids: Revell, 2002), 40–43. Fleming H. Revell is a division of Baker Publishing Group.

80 Adapted from Brother Andrew with Verne Becker, *The Calling* (Grand Rapids: Revell, 2002), 125–128. Fleming H. Revell is a division of Baker Publishing Group.

81 See John 16:33; Matthew 5:10–12; James 1:2–4.

82 See John 1:42–43; Matthew 16:17–19.

83 See Luke 8:51–56; Matthew 17:1–8; 26:36–46.

84 See Matthew 16:21–23; John 13:31–38.

85 See Matthew 26:47–58, 69–75; John 18:1–27.

86 See John 21:1–23.

87 See Acts 2–4; 5:12–42; 9:31–11:18; 12:1–24; 15:1–33; Galatians 2.

88 See 2 Peter 1:16–21.

89 "As he thinks within himself, so he is" (Proverbs 23:7, NASB).

90 See John 10:10.